The
125
Most Asked Questions
About Horses
. . . and the Answers

THE

125

MOST ASKED QUESTIONS

ABOUT HORSES

...AND THE ANSWERS

JOHN MALONE

WILLIAM MORROW AND COMPANY, INC.

NEW YORK

Library of Congress Cataloging-in-Publication Data

Malone, John Williams.
    The 125 most asked questions about horses . . . and the answers / by John Malone.
      p. cm.
    Includes bibliographical references (p.   ) and index.
    ISBN 0-688-11312-5
    1. Horses—Miscellanea. 2. Horsemanship—Miscellanea. 3. Horse sports—Miscellanea. I. Title. II. Title: One hundred twenty-five most asked questions about horses (and the answers).
SF285.M25   1994
636.1—dc20   93-40777
                                                      CIP

Printed in the United States of America

First Edition

1 2 3 4 5 6 7 8 9 10

BOOK DESIGN BY PATRICE FODERO

ILLUSTRATIONS BY LISA STOKES

CONTENTS

I.

THE FIRST RIDERS

Q. Since the greatest number of horse breeds exist in Europe, I have always assumed that that is where riding first began. But a friend who is a historian says that is doubtful, and that the earliest evidence suggests that riding developed in the Middle East. *Why wouldn't riding have begun earlier in Europe than in the Middle East?*

A. There are two main reasons, one involving climate and terrain and the other reflecting the rise of civilization. The true horse, known as *Equus caballus,* developed out of a much smaller animal called the *Eohippus,* which existed as far back as sixty million years ago. Exactly when the first true horses evolved, probably in the high steppes of Eastern Europe, is an unsettled question. There is evidence that horses were being eaten by early man in Europe, but is unlikely that they were ridden because so much of Europe was then either heavily forested or very swampy. As agriculture did not exist, there would have been no reason to put horses to work.

Civilization arose in the Middle East with the beginnings of agriculture, and it is from what used to be known as Persia, now Iran, that the earliest concrete evidence of horseback riding exists in the form of primitive drawings and figurines. Riding appears to have originated sometime around 3000 B.C.

2.

COLD BLOOD, HOT BLOOD, WARM BLOOD

Q. I am confused. I was always taught that mammals were warm-blooded creatures, biologically speaking, while birds and reptiles were cold-blooded. But I have recently learned that there are three kinds of horses: cold-blooded, warm-blooded, and hot-blooded. *To what extent, if any, do the terms cold-, warm-, and hot-blooded reflect biological differences in horses?*

A. The differences are not the kind we think of in distinguishing mammals and reptiles, but distinct genetic differences between these three types of horses. The terms cold, warm, and hot are applied to horses in a more general, even metaphorical way, distinguishing between the heavy-boned horses of northern Europe (cold-blooded), the sleeker horses of the Mediterranean and Middle East (hot-blooded), and the intermediate type (warm-blooded), which may have developed independently or may have arisen as a cross between the northern and southern types.

3.

A COMMON ANCESTOR?

Q. A great many of the well-known horse breeds seem to have developed in the past two centuries. I know that some breeds of ponies and horses, like the Shetland pony and the pure Arabian, go back much farther than that. *Are there any breeds of horses that have been around long enough to be considered possible ancestors to just about all other breeds?*

A. The most likely candidate is the Mongolian Wild Horse, also known as the *Przewalskii,* after Colonel N. M. Przewalski, the first European to discover it (in 1881). This extremely hardy horse, with a ponylike head, still exists in the mountains to the west of the Gobi Desert. It is under the protection of the Mongolian, Russian, and Chinese governments, but its numbers in the wild are believed to be small, perhaps exceeded by the 250 or so that are in zoos. It should be said that some experts are dubious about the Przewalskii being a common ancestor to most breeds because of its unusual chromosome count—which others take as evidence of its antiquity.

Another candidate is the Tarpan, now found in Poland but earlier found over a much greater range. There are arguments here because of evidence that at the end of the last century the Polish government made an effort to preserve the breed by crossing it with very similar horses. Even if that is true, the horses that do exist are regarded as extremely close to the original Ice Age ancestor.

4.

EXTINCT IN NORTH AMERICA

Q. It is well known that there were no horses on the North American continent when the first Europeans landed five hundred years ago, and that the horses used so effectively by the Plains Indians were the descendants of escaped Spanish horses. *How long ago was it that the horses indigenous to North America became extinct?*

A. It was only in the last fifty thousand years that the original horses of North America, as well as its elephants, rhinos, and camels, became extinct. There is some question about how and why these extinctions took place. The last ice age was certainly a factor, since it changed the climate dramatically. But many experts believe that there were remnants of these various breeds still roaming the central and lower United States when the peoples who had crossed over the Bering Land Bridge from Asia began to populate North America some forty thousand years ago. It is generally agreed that the remaining horses and other animals were then hunted into final extinction by various tribespeople who were making their way south into Central America and beyond.

5.
A HORSE IS A HORSE
IS A HORSE

Q. Most people seem to assume that the smartest of all domestic animals is the dog, and that even a pig is smarter than a horse. Perhaps I am prejudiced, being the owner of several horses, but I find it difficult to believe this ranking. *Don't horses have a far better memory than any other domestic animals?*

A. Horses have prodigious memories of a situational kind, but there are old arguments and crucial misunderstandings at work here. A horse's brain is remarkably small, but that really doesn't have much to do with intelligence—if we go by brain size, we might as well agree that whales are much smarter than we are. The real problem is the human desire to anthropomorphize animals—to attribute human qualities to them. This is simply foolish with regard to the horse; it is a creature of instinct, not reason. It is much more reasonable to attribute human qualities to dogs. (And when it comes to pigs, the great English poet Robert Herrick had a sow that lived in his house, and there is some evidence that his immortal love sonnets to "Julia" were in fact addressed to her!)

One of the reasons that people insist that horses are dumb is that these magnificent animals so completely resist our efforts to give them human characteristics. More power to them.

6.

AN UNNATURAL BURDEN?

Q. I have a friend who says that horses were never meant to be ridden and that it's unnatural for them to carry that much weight on their backs. This woman is something of an animal rights fanatic, and I tend to discount a good many of her pronouncements. *Is it really unnatural for a horse to carry a rider?*

A. We've all seen westerns in which stunts are performed with Indians or cowboys clinging to the underbelly of a horse. In fact, from the horse's point of view, that is the easiest way to carry weight. It is also why the positioning of a rider astride a horse—the distribution of the rider's weight—is so important, and should vary depending upon what task a horse is being asked to perform. This is not because the back itself is weak, but because wrongly distributed weight can so easily injure the horse's legs by forcing an unnatural gait. Poor weight distribution also creates a high risk of damage to a horse's kidneys.

Still, it is going too far to say that horses were never meant to be ridden. They must simply be ridden correctly.

7.

PONDERING HORSEPOWER

Q. My car is listed as having two hundred horsepower, and can easily tow a large RV trailer. Apparently some draft horses can move several tons of cut-down trees, which is a lot more than my car could accomplish. *Exactly what does horsepower measure and how can a horse exceed one horsepower?*

A. The term *horsepower* was coined by the eighteenth-century Scottish inventor James Watt, who developed the first

practical steam engine and also gave his name to the electrical term *wattage*. He was as far as you can get from the absent-minded professor and had a keen grasp of the larger world. His invention of the unit of measure he called horsepower was essentially a public-relations ploy. He knew the average person would not grasp or be convinced by scientific drawings of his steam engine, and so sought to put its power in terms readily understood by most people. Thus, horsepower.

Watt used real horses to determine that a horse could raise a 550-pound weight by one foot per second—a rate that a horse could maintain over a ten-hour workday. Thus, even though he experimented with real horses, the rates he ended up using do not correspond to what a horse can accomplish at peak performance over a shorter period. For instance, it has been calculated that a horse going over a jump can put out a burst of energy equal to thirty or forty horsepower. No horse can keep this up for long, of course. Horsepower as a unit of measurement pertains to the amount of constant effort sustained over a given period of time. In a brief period a real horse can do a great deal more, including moving tons of logs over a small stretch of ground.

8.

THE MYSTERY OF THE STIRRUP

Q. One of the pleasures of watching a movie like *Dances with Wolves* is seeing horses being ridden bareback without stirrups by Native Americans. *How long ago were stirrups first used and where did it happen?*

A. The oldest stirrups ever found date back to the fourth century B.C. in western China. Why it should have taken so long to develop such an obvious aid to riding is something that greatly puzzles historians. It is possible that leather stirrups may have been used earlier, but they disintegrated, leaving no record for historians.

Whether they were invented in the fourth century B.C. or earlier, stirrups were not widely used for centuries. In England, for example, stirrups weren't used until the sixth century, two hundred years after the first appearance there of the uprising "tree" at the front of the saddle, a less important development in terms of horsemanship.

9.

LEGENDARY ARABIANS

Q. I have been told that the most selectively bred horse in the history of the world is the Arabian. *When were Arabians first bred?*

A. The breeding of Arabians dates back at least to the seventh century, to the time of Mohammed, who commanded in the Koran that these horses be treated with exceptional care. While the Arabian is probably, like most horses, descended from the wild horses of the European steppes, the desert environment in which it lived, as well as the fanatical breeding efforts of the Bedouin tribes of the Middle East, produced a horse like no other.

Because of the harshness of desert life and the sparsity of forage, the Arabian was fed a diet that would give most horses an instant case of colic: camel's milk, the dried meat of camels, dates, and even locusts. The Bedouin obsession with purity of line, which they call *asil,* also led to a program of inbreeding that is the antithesis of the approach taken by Western horse breeders. But instead of the usual problems of deterioration of the breed associated with inbreeding, this approach has helped maintain the legendary strength of the Arabian largely because of extremely strict rules of breeding. There is a famous, and true, story of a rider who carried the message of a Russian defeat nearly a hundred miles in a single day. The rider died as a result, but the horse, named Omar Pasha, showed no ill effects.

10.

NATIVE·AMERICAN BRED

Q. We have just moved to Wyoming from the East Coast, and are very taken by the Appaloosa horses that are so common here. I had always thought that the Appaloosa was essentially a cowboy horse, but people around here say it was developed by Native Americans. *What is the actual history of the Appaloosa?*

A. The Appaloosa was greatly favored by cowboys, but there is little question that it was initially bred by the Nez Percé Indians of Oregon, southern Washington, and western Idaho. Like many of the western breeds, its ancestors were most likely Span-

ish horses brought over in the sixteenth century. But the Nez Percé bred their horses selectively to produce the strikingly spotted Appaloosa, named after the Palouse River of the region.

The Nez Percé, who had always gotten along well with white settlers, from Lewis and Clark on, resisted being confined to reservations in the mid-1870s, and their numbers were drastically reduced in a famous series of battles in 1877. But the horse they had bred for its stamina, good disposition, and beguiling appearance went on to become one of the most appreciated of American breeds. Fully recognized as a separate breed since the late 1930s, true Appaloosas come in six patterns, ranging from the leopard to the spotted blanket.

11.

GO FIGURE THE MORGAN

Q. To my mind, the Morgan is the best all-round horse of the American breeds. I know it was named for a New England schoolteacher named Justin Morgan. *How did Mr. Morgan go about developing the breed that bears his name?*

A. He didn't, or least not intentionally. This is the kind of story that would strain credulity if it appeared in a novel. Justin Morgan was a most interesting man, to be sure; like many Americans of his time, Justin Morgan was a man of many abilities—schoolteacher and farmer, musician, and admirer of horses. In 1795, he accepted a horse named Figure in payment for a debt. Figure was used on his Vermont farm, raced occasionally, pulled a carriage on Sundays, and earned Justin Morgan some extra income as a sire. After Justin Morgan's death, the new owner took less care of the horse and used him more harshly. Figure was eventually killed by wolves in the winter of 1821.

It soon became apparent that Figure had sired a remarkable number of first-rate horses during his lifetime, and they in turn produced more offspring of stature. Since Figure's own ancestry was obscure, the breed became known as the Morgan horse. Handsome, hardy, and strong, Morgan horses are to this day regarded as one of the world's top-notch all-round breeds.

12.

FROM STRENGTH TO STRENGTH

Q. I'm aware that the American Quarter Horse is regarded as the best there is when it comes to herding cattle. A friend of mine who recently invested in a small ranch says these horses seem to have a sixth sense about what cattle will do next. *Was the American Quarter Horse especially bred for cattle ranching?*

A. No, the American Quarter Horse had been fully established for well over a century before cattle ranching became a major force in the western states. As its name implies, it was originally bred for short races, usually a quarter of a mile. It can put on a burst of speed from a standing start that would put any Thoroughbred to shame—essential in such a short race. The breed was first developed in Virginia and the Carolinas during the first half of the seventeenth century, when various types of mares brought over by the Spaniards were crossed with English stallions.

By the time Thoroughbred racing had started to supplant Quarter-Horse racing, it was discovered that the quick burst of speed made possible by the Quarter Horse's massive hindquarters was perfect for controlling cattle on the move, and the breed's agility and intelligence only added to its value. In the last two decades there has been a considerable revival of Quarter-Horse racing, and the breed is also highly valued as a pleasure horse. As a result, it has become the most popular breed of horse in the world.

13.
A UNIQUE GAIT

Q. I love to watch the high-stepping running walk of the Tennessee Walking Horse. I know these horses were bred for the comfortable action or gait by southern plantation owners at the end of the last century. *Is the unique running walk of the Tennessee Walking Horse something that owners were particularly looking for in their breeding programs, or was it mostly a piece of genetic luck?*

A. The main object of the plantation owners was to produce a horse with an exceptionally smooth action. The breed has three gaits that make it unique. The first is a basically ordinary walk,

but a very fluid one, that show horses can be trained to combine with a characteristic cadenced turning of the head from side to side that is a delight to watch. The second gait—and what was particularly being sought by plantation owners—is a canter marked by a wonderful ease and length of stride. The third gait, the high-stepping running walk, was a dividend that owners no doubt sought to preserve and enhance once they had seen it in action. It is a unique gait—trainers have tried to teach it to a number of other breeds without success. In fact, it is now so deeply inbred that foals often start doing it simply in imitation of their dams, with no intervention from humans whatsoever.

14.

SKEWED PINTOS?

Q. As an Oklahoma native, I am very partial to Pintos, which are so common in my state. I was surprised to discover on a visit to England that horses with Pinto markings are referred to by the derogatory names "skewbalds" or "piebalds." *Why do the English look down on horses of the Pinto type?*

A. The terms *skewbald* and *piebald* are centuries old, and they were very likely somewhat derogatory in their origin since these horses were much favored by gypsies and tinkers, who stood very low on the class ladder. But although the names have survived (to the annoyance of Americans like you), Pintos are now very popular in England, where they are cherished for the many sterling characteristics that once made them one of the primary horses of Native Americans of the Great Plains, including stamina, courage, and loyalty.

15.

WAR HORSES

Q. A friend has told me that the ancestors of the Clydesdale horses that we see in Budweiser advertisements were used as war horses a few hundred years ago. The Clydesdales are certainly beautiful animals in their way, but they seem far too heavy and slow to be of much use in battle. *Was the Clydesdale really bred originally as a war horse?*

A. The Clydesdale, along with such survivors as the English Suffolk Punch and the Shire, were indeed originally bred as war horses. Their very heaviness was the point. They were among a class of horse throughout Europe that were called *Great Horses,*

21

specifically bred to carry the massively armored knights of the Middle Ages. Not only did they have to bear the weight of a man wearing as much as a hundred pounds of armor, but also the burden of up to eighty pounds of armor on their own bodies. Of course this was ultimately a self-defeating form of warfare. The horses moved so slowly that winning the battle largely depended upon knocking a man off his horse, which he was too weighed down to remount.

The spreading use of muskets brought an abrupt end to the use of the Great Horse in battle. As speed and maneuverability became paramount, the Great Horses and their descendants were relegated to the role of draft horses, pulling plows and wagons, for which they were much better suited in the first place.

16.

THE MOST POPULAR HEAVYWEIGHT

Q. Among draft horses, Clydesdales and Percherons seem to get all the publicity as the "glamour" breeds of heavy horses. But in the Midwest, where I live, the draft horses of preference are the Belgians. You can find them on half a dozen farms within ten miles of my home. *How do Belgians actually stack up in popularity with other draft horses in the United States?*

A. They are vastly more popular than any of them. There are about five times as many registered Belgians as all other draft breeds put together! Originally a cross between two of the most ancient heavy horses, the Belgian Ardennes and the Brabant, Belgians have a breed registry in America that goes all the way back to 1887. These are working horses of the highest order, and beauties as well. One of the tallest of horses, often reaching nineteen hands, they can pull anything from a family cart to tons of logs. They are also gentle and affectionate, easygoing giants of the horse world.

Belgians have long suffered from a certain degree of snobbery in the horse world, however. Most European books on horses don't even mention them. But that may be changing—they are beginning to be imported to Belgium itself.

17.

FINO AS IN SMOOTH

Q. Many people claim that the smoothest riding horse around is the Tennessee Walking Horse. I would have agreed until I had my first ride on a Paso Fino while on a visit to Puerto Rico. *How well known is the Paso Fino on the U.S. mainland?*

A. It is becoming increasingly well known, although the owners and breeders of this splendid horse would just as soon it didn't become *too* popular. They tend to talk about it in the hushed terms usually reserved for a favorite small restaurant or out-of-the-way country inn. But they will all tell you that the Paso Fino is the smoothest riding horse in the world. They just can't help boasting.

It is believed that the Paso Fino is a direct descendant of Spanish horses brought to the New World by Columbus and subsequent explorers for Spain. Those horses were Andalusians, Barbs, and the Spanish Jennets. The Jennet, now extinct, is probably responsible for the unique lateral four-beat gaits of these horses. The Paso Fino has three natural gaits—the *paso fino,* the *paso corto,* and the *paso largo,* each faster than the next. The paso fino gait is a walk, while the paso corto and paso largo can be roughly compared to a trot and a canter. Actually they are neither, and offer a motion that is quite special, involving very little vertical motion of the shoulder, and hence an exceptionally smooth ride.

These are natural gaits, and a true Paso Fino will exhibit the gaits shortly after birth. These gaits may be refined with training, but other horses cannot be trained to duplicate the movement. The breed is centered on the Caribbean, Puerto Rico, and Colombia, and there is a very similar horse known as the Peruvian Paso Fino. There are only a few thousand breeders and owners in the United States, but it is doubtful they will be able to keep their secret much longer.

18.

A NEW BREED

Q. A friend has purchased a National Show Horse for her daughter. This sounds to me like a generic term, but I am told it is a specific breed. *How long has the National Show Horse been around and what sets it apart from other breeds?*

A. The National Show Horse is a cross between the Arabian and the American Saddlebred breeds. It was established very recently, with a registry inaugurated in 1982. The first national competition for the breed was established in the same year. The range of competitive categories, all of which offer prize money, has expanded considerably in the brief history of the breed, and now extends from halter through western to ladies' sidesaddle classes.

There are now more than 10,000 registered horses, with the number growing every year. The National Show Horse Registry has placed special emphasis on recruiting young riders, and awards college scholarships to top competitors. Becoming involved with a new breed always offers special challenges and a splendid sense of comradery among owners and competitors. Put that together with the unusual attention given to young riders, and your friend's daughter can consider herself a fortunate young lady.

19.

A COLOR, NOT A BREED

Q. My grandson was given a horse for his twelfth birthday. Both he and his father refer to it as a Palomino, but it's quite a small horse, and as someone who grew up watching Roy Rogers and his famous horse Trigger, I wonder if they've been taken for a ride. *Can a true Palomino be small in stature?*

A. You are making a common but mistaken assumption. The Palomino is not a breed, but simply a particular coloration. To be considered a true Palomino, a horse must have a golden coat, with no white marking except on the face or legs, and the mane and tail should be white. Thus horses of quite different sizes and even conformation can be called Palominos. The Palominos most favored in the United States are Quarter Horses, but in Great Britain they are much more likely to be ponies.

There are those who would like to see the development and recognition of a Palomino breed, but since even achieving the proper coloration, never mind conformation, is tricky, it seems unlikely that will happen.

20.
DONKEY PREJUDICE

Q. We live in an area of Pennsylvania that is considered serious horse country. But we don't have horses, we have two donkeys. This means that even though we live in a beautiful restored 1830's farmhouse, we tend to get treated as though we were denizens of a trailer park. Okay, I can understand the snobbery. But what I can't understand is why so many horse people seem almost afraid of donkeys. Our two fellas like to be petted on the head, but when they put their heads down and lay their ears back for a nice scratch, horse people jump back like they've been snarled at by a vicious dog. *Why are so many horse people nervous about donkeys?*

A. The answer lies in your question—and while your horse-owner friends need to learn more about donkeys, you also need to learn more about horses. When a horse puts its ears back, it is a sign that it is very upset, and may do anything from rearing to kicking, or biting. To horse people, laid-back ears are a sign of danger, one that means get out of the way fast. That's not true of donkeys, but many people who own horses know little about the difference between horses and donkeys.

Certainly, though, your horse-owner friends are also harboring all kinds of prejudices. It doesn't matter that Mary rode a donkey into Jerusalem, or that donkeys were instrumental to the well-being of armies from the time of the Crusades right up through World War I. Donkeys are, to use the terminology of Vietnam veterans, the "grunts" of the horse world, along with the even more maligned mule. There are many people who know their donkeys and mules, and their horses as well, who will tell you unequivocally that donkeys are more intelligent than horses, and that the poor sterile mule—offspring of a jack donkey and a horse mare—is the smartest of the lot. But horse people don't want to hear it; why, their animals *cost* so much more, and they can win million-dollar purses, and do dressage and win Olympic medals, I mean, after all . . .

Donkeys are wonderful animals, and as to the mule, when the jeep was first put into service, that tough old general named Patton marveled that it could do anything a mule could, just faster. Keep your chin up, but understand you are championing a permanent underclass. So long as *you* know how terrific your donkeys are, does it really matter what other people think?

21.

WILD MUSTANGS

Q. The Mustangs of the American West, as I understand it, are descended from Spanish horses that either escaped or were stolen by Indians. I had thought, however, that the Spanish horses of the seventeenth century were quite elegant animals, and the Mustangs certainly are not. *Did Mustangs become what they are because they were interbred with inferior horses?*

A.   It is now believed that the Mustangs became a distinct breed as a result of natural selection. Many authorities speak of them as having degenerated, but in an evolutionary sense that is unfair. They roamed wild over a vast area, much of it extremely inhospitable country, and only the toughest strains survived. In terms of evolutionary behavior, they adapted rather than degenerated. Extremely tough, they have among the hardest hooves of any horses, and very seldom fall lame.

Although Mustangs are by nature quite intractable, the Native-American tribes of the West, and later the cowboys, learned to break them. Because of their toughness and stamina they often put the Indians at an advantage in battles with United States Cavalry, since the army horses were better bred but not nearly as hardy. Mustangs were for a while in danger of dying out as a breed, but protected lands have been set aside for them in several states, where they continue to run wild as they have for centuries.

22.

SWIMMING THE CHANNEL

Q. One of my favorite books as a child was *Misty of Chincoteague.* *Are the wild ponies of Chincoteague still rounded up and auctioned every year?*

A. The main wild herd of Chincoteague ponies, about 250 in number, actually live on Assateague. These two small islands off the coast of Maryland and Virginia are separated by a narrow channel, and on the last Thursday of July each year, the Assateague ponies are rounded up and at low tide made to swim across the channel to be branded. A certain number are sold at auction, because otherwise the herd would become too large for the marshland of Assateague to support. Thousands of people turn out every year to see the spectacle of the ponies swimming across the channel on Thursday or being returned to their home on Friday.

The origin of these ponies is a total mystery, although one popular legend holds that they were aboard a Moorish vessel that was wrecked off the islands. It is quite probable that they lived on the islands for nearly two centuries before anyone realized they were there. While they are termed ponies, they have the build of a small horse and do not have a typical pony head. Like the Mustang of the American West, they clearly must have evolved to survive in their harsh environment.

23.

HOW MANY HANDS?

Q. It has always struck me as odd that a horse's height is measured in *hands.* Since the size of human hands can vary considerably, even in adults, the use of the term seems awfully

29

imprecise. *Does a hand have a specific equivalent in inches or centimeters?*

A.   A hand is four inches. This is one of those measurements that was established long ago and is now a convention. The measurement is taken from the ground to the highest point of the horse's back at the withers, where the neck and the back are joined. To convert from hands to inches, multiply the number of hands by four. If a horse stands 15.2 hands high, multiply 15 by 4, and then add the number following the decimal point: thus, 62 inches. Strict mathematics are not being followed here, since the .2 is not a percentage of a full hand, but rather indicates each inch beyond a hand.

If an animal stands less than 14.2 hands high at the withers, it is not a horse but a pony.

24.

HORSESHOE HISTORY

Q.   I am curious about the practice of shoeing horses. Obviously, wild horses aren't shod, and as I understand it, nailed-on horseshoes only go back about 1,500 years. There were armies on horseback long before that. *When did shoeing begin, and is it really as necessary as we are led to believe?*

A.   So far as we know, the first horseshoes were used by the Greeks, but they were more like moccasins than modern horseshoes. In the last century B.C., the Greeks fashioned horseshoes by cutting circles of rawhide with holes punched around the perimeter through which a drawstring could be woven. Later they added a metal plate to the bottom of this foot pouch. The Romans initially used the same device, but as they laid down paved roads, they began molding an iron "sandal" around the hoof.

The nailed-on iron horseshoe probably dates from the end of

the fourth century, although direct evidence of its use in the form of an actual shoe doesn't exist further back than the end of the following century. Of course, the use of iron developed at different periods in different parts of the world. Thus the great Native-American riders of the Plains were using rawhide boots as late as the nineteenth century—although they often did not even use those, since their horses had extremely tough hooves.

These days aluminum shoes are used for racehorses, dressage performers, and other show horses, while work horses that must deal with hard surfaces are often given rubber shoes. Special shoes of many different conformations are employed for horses with problem hooves of various kinds.

Is all this necessary? There are those who point to the Mustangs and wonder. But wild Mustangs make their own rules, while we use horses for so many specialized tasks and sporting events, and work them so hard, that protective shoeing is usually a necessity. It can go too far, perhaps, with some horses being fitted with the equivalent of high heels to promote a particular gait. In most cases, though, shoes are essential.

25.
SHOEING IT RIGHT

Q. There's a farrier in our area who has a great reputation and charges a bundle. But so far as my experience goes, he is either careless or doesn't really know what he's doing. A horse I took to him was so badly shod that the job had to be redone by someone else two weeks later. *Aren't there any certification requirements for farriers?*

A. Unfortunately, no. Just as you can say, "I'm a writer," even though you've never sold so much as a sentence, so too can you set yourself up in business shoeing horses. An unpublished writer can't do much harm, but an amateur farrier can wreak havoc on prized horses.

There is, however, an organization that *does* certify farriers. The Brotherhood of Working Farriers Association certifies eleven levels of expertise from Apprentice to Master. To achieve the top level requires not only a top-notch demonstration of skills, but also years of practical experience—as many as fifteen for those who apply and have not gradually worked their way up through the ranks, and even by that route it will take seven years. The standards of the BWFA are exacting, and the certificates issued at the various levels clearly state what the holder is accredited to do.

Of course, there are farriers who aren't going to bother with this and are still masters of their craft—farriers who were taught by their parents, who were taught by theirs, are likely to know exactly what they are doing. But if you have doubts, ask about BWFA certification.

26.

TRIMMING HOOVES

Q. I remove my horse's shoes to trim the new growth of horn about every six weeks. My brother, who has owned a horse much longer than I have, tells me that I should be doing it every four weeks. *Am I being lax in trimming my horse's hooves at six-week intervals?*

A. You are adhering to a schedule that the majority of horse owners use. But different horses have different horn growth rates. The difference can be as much as a half inch a month, the average being between a quarter inch and three-quarters of an inch. With a new horse, it is advisable to use a four-week inspection schedule to make sure everything is all right. Once you have a clear understanding of how fast your own horse grows new horn, fix on a regular schedule that seems appropriate, whether it is four weeks, five weeks, six weeks, or even more. Your brother may be correct in trimming his horse's hooves every four weeks, but you may be correct in your own schedule for your own horse.

27.
BOTHERSOME BRANDING

Q. On a recent trip out west, we were privileged to watch some horses being branded. At least my husband and son thought it was a privilege. I found it inhumane and painful to watch. *Is branding as brutal as it looks, and is there any real reason to do it?*

A. There are several different forms of branding. Fire branding is traditional in the American West, dating from the great trail-driving days following the Civil War, with such famous brands as the King Ranch's "Running W," the "Rocking Chair" brand, and the "Quarter Circle T." With a properly hot branding iron, the process should last only a few seconds, and is not as traumatic to the horse as it looks. These days a freeze brand is often used, making use of a copper branding instrument (because of its conductivity) that is frozen in a mixture of dry ice and mentholated spirits. This is less painful, but the horse must be restrained longer, for about 25-35 seconds depending on the color of the coat. This form of branding causes the hairs to grow in white in the shape of the brand, which can be seen as much as 120 feet away.

Finally, there is lip branding, which is really tattooing, used on Thoroughbreds and show horses to avoid marring their coats. Because the lips are so sensitive, this process requires a local anesthetic.

There are several legal reasons for branding. Horses do get stolen, some horses look so much alike that a brand is really the only way to tell them apart and, in terms of racing, branding prevents horses from being switched to score betting coups.

28.

SADDLE SHAPES

Q. The various kinds of saddles, from the very small saddles you see on show horses to the heavy and sometimes highly decorated western saddles, are obviously used for very different tasks. But I have never understood whether the differences in saddles have to do with the comfort of the rider or the control of the horse. *Is saddle shape determined more by the horse's needs or the rider's needs?*

A. A good saddle should be comfortable to both horse and rider. The primary purpose of a saddle, no matter the shape, is the proper distribution of the rider's weight for the job that the horse is being asked to perform. The horse's center of gravity is all-important here, but the center of gravity shifts according to the kind of task the horse is carrying out. Thus, a dressage saddle places the weight of the rider farther back than usual, giving the horse freer use of its forelegs. The weight of the rider moves the horse's center of gravity to the rear. The jumping saddle does exactly the opposite, moving the horse's center of gravity forward since the animal's rear legs must provide the power for a jump.

Western saddles are somewhat different. Since western riders usually spend long hours in the saddle, the comfort of the rider becomes more important. But since these saddles weigh so much, the use of a saddle blanket is particularly important for the comfort of the horse.

29.

ABOUT THAT BIT

Q. My fourteen-year-old daughter has been riding since she was ten, and has had her own horse for eight months. She rides for pleasure, and is not involved in showing or jumping, but she has suddenly gotten it into her head that she needs an entirely different kind of bit for her horse. I am not objecting to the expense involved, but I don't want her getting something more complicated than the jointed egg-butt snaffle bit she has simply because some other girl has one. *Is there any need for an ordinary riding horse to be fitted with a complex form of bit?*

A. There shouldn't be. Snaffle bits (and there are several types of these) are the most commonly used and should be adequate for a pleasure horse. More complicated forms of bit are used for one of two reasons; either to correct a problem in the horse's behavior or to give the rider additional control during demanding maneuvers such as jumping. Thus, a rearing bit might be used with a yearling colt that tends to be wayward. Trainers of show-jumping horses are constantly experimenting with bits in order to help the rider fine-tune communication of complex commands to the horse.

The bit, in other words, should conform to the situation. In your daughter's case, I think you have reason to suspect that an element of "keeping up with the Joneses" has entered into the picture. Unless she is having a problem with her horse, a snaffle bit should do the job just fine.

30.

A ROOM WITH A VIEW

Q. We have moved from the city to the country, and are
planning to buy one or two horses. There is an old barn on our
property, but it is in bad repair, so we will have to do a major job
on it. *What kind of stabling requirements should we consider?*

A. Most horse experts recommend a loose box rather than a
narrow stall of the older type, in which a horse can barely lie
down. A minimum of twelve feet by twelve feet is best, with a
roof twelve feet high (if possible) in order to increase air circu-
lation. Some breeders and owners swear by concrete floors, others
prefer wood, and some champion packed dirt. Those who are
against concrete note that it is slippery both to horse and human,
although that can be compensated for by deeper bedding. Wood,
of course, will rot, but leaving air space between the wood and the
ground can slow decay. Dirt floors will need to be turned over,
more dirt added, and packed down again about every six
months—more work, but some feel best for the horse.
   Most experts agree that stalls should have a double door, with
a top and a bottom. The top is usually left open to cut down on
boredom, which can lead to many kinds of mischief and down-
right neuroticism. You will see barns owned by professional
breeders in which the horses are kept in narrow stalls which they
can hardly see out of at all, but that kind of arrangement is
increasingly discouraged.
   When using a double door, the bottom must rise high enough
so the horse can't jump over it, but it shouldn't be so high that the
horse can't stick its head out. Even horses need a room with a
view.

31.

BEDDING CHOICES

Q. As new horse owners, we are getting a lot of advice from other owners, some of it conflicting. For example, some people say that the best bedding for horses is straw, others swear by wood shavings. And both sides have dire stories about the consequences of making the wrong choice. *Is the choice between straw and wood shavings for a horse's bedding really of that much importance?*

A. The reason this argument exists is that both straw and wood shavings have advantages and disadvantages. Straw is easier to handle because it comes in bales and can be removed with a pitchfork. It is also comfortable for the horse, gives good insulation (particularly important if the floor beneath it is concrete), and it absorbs urine without matting badly. The drawback: some horses regard straw as a between-meal snack, and if they eat too much of it they may develop impaction colic.

Wood shavings also make a comfortable bed, but need to be more thickly applied since they do not absorb urine as well. Horses don't eat wood shavings, which is an advantage, but shavings tend to collect on the sole of the hoof, causing other problems.

These days, many horse owners are experimenting with other bedding materials, or combinations of them. There is, for instance, a vogue for finely crushed peanut shells. Other horse owners use a layer of paper on top of straw, wood shavings, or peanut shells. The advantage to this is that the urine-soaked top layer of paper can be easily lifted off, and the underbedding raked and occasionally refreshed. You could also finesse the recommendations of your advisors by using an underlayer of wood shavings and a top layer of straw.

32.

SAFETY IN RUBBER AND PLASTIC

Q. I recently bought a horse, which I am boarding at a farm about a mile away. Everything seems fine about the place, with one exception. The stall is roomy, but it is equipped with a galvanized tin feed bin and water bucket. *Aren't rubber or plastic bins and buckets a much better idea?*

A. Yes, they are, but some old-timers resist them. The problem with galvanized tin, of course, is that a horse can hurt itself by banging against the feed box, or by kicking over the bucket and getting a hoof caught between the handle and the bucket. A horse with a bucket on its foot is like a dog with a tin can tied to its tail: frantic. Serious injury can result.

Whether rubber or tin, the water bucket should be securely fastened in some way, so that it can't be kicked over. A horse without water is a horse in distress. The owner of the barn where you are boarding your horse may mutter about ''newfangled ideas,'' but if you volunteer to pay for everything, he will probably come around.

33.

GROOMING MUSCLES

Q. We have agreed to buy a horse for our nine-year-old son with the understanding that he will do everything required to take care of it. Some friends think we are being unrealistic, saying that there is more to the job of caring for a horse than we recognize, and that our son may not even be strong enough yet to do a proper job of grooming. *Does grooming a horse really require all that much strength?*

A. There's no reason why a nine-year-old boy can't care for a horse properly—farm kids do it all the time. But the job is time-consuming and requires a lot of hard work. Make sure he knows what he is in for. As to the question of grooming, it does require a lot of energy, but not all that much physical strength. The problem is that many first-time horse owners don't recognize that a nice, gentle brushing down that makes the horse look good is not enough. Thorough grooming has the objective of soothing a horse's muscles, not just cleaning its skin. If a horse is being properly groomed, the person doing it is going to work up a good sweat, even in cold weather. Your son is likely to be sore when he finishes grooming his horse, particularly at the beginning, but in the process he will also be building up his own muscles. And he'll be doing it in a far more natural way than is possible at any gym or fitness center.

34.
WOODEN FENCES

Q. I've bought a "fixer-upper" farm with five acres of pastureland divided into three sections by barbed-wire fences. This seemed perfect for a couple of horses, but I'm being told to wait on buying horses until I replace the barbed wire with wooden fencing, an expensive proposition. *Is it really necessary to have wooden fences instead of barbed wire for horses?*

A. It is *very* important. Barbed wire is fine for cattle, but a disaster for horses. In the Old West, the cattle-grazing pastures were surrounded by barbed wire. But horse enclosures were always wood, even in areas where it was scarce. The problem is that horses can be "spooked" by anything from a low-flying owl to a clap of thunder. In panic, they will try to run for the hills, and if there is barbed wire in the way, they can suffer puncture wounds that can lead to anything from tetanus to peritonitis.

You not only have to have wooden (or fiberglass) fences, but they must be strong, too high to jump over easily, with a rail low enough to the ground so that colts or smaller horses can't squeeze under them. You no doubt know the expression, "If you have to ask the price you can't afford it." Well, in the horse world, "If you can't afford a wooden fence, you can't afford a horse."

35.

PONY HARDINESS

Q. We are considering buying a Shetland pony. A couple of owners we have talked with say that we won't have to worry about stabling, that they leave their Shetlands out in the open year round. While we live in southern Oregon, which is a fairly temperate place, we are dubious about this. *Is it really all right to leave a pony outdoors on pastureland the year round?*

A. Some ponies of certain breeds, the Shetland among them, really do better spending the entire year in the open. But there are a number of issues to consider before making a decision.

First, many ponies, particularly the British breeds (also including the Welsh, Exmoor, New Forest, and others) are of the northern, cold-blooded strains that have roamed the higher elevations of Great Britain from time immemorial. They are enormously hardy, and can stand temperatures that horses with warm-blooded ancestry (even in part) simply can't cope with. In a state like Oregon, with a climate quite similar to that of the British Isles, a Shetland is likely to thrive in the open. But in states such as Wyoming or New York, where deep snow and howling blizzards are common, the pony should really be brought in during really cold or stormy weather.

Even in Oregon, however, you are going to have to provide additional food in the form of hay. And as always, water must be plentiful. Keep in mind that water in a trough will freeze more quickly and harder than that in a flowing stream. The fact that a pony can be very happy living outdoors year round does not mean in any way that it can be left to fend entirely for itself. This is especially true if it does not have the companionship of other ponies. If you and another owner or two could work out an arrangement to have your ponies share a pasture, all the animals would be better off.

36.

GALLOP FIRST, FEED AFTER

Q. After much pleading, my grandson, who's thirteen, was given a horse for his birthday. When visiting recently, I was alarmed to discover that in the mornings he was going out and feeding his horse and then taking him for a gallop before going off to school. *Shouldn't a horse be fed after exercising rather than before?*

A. Absolutely! No horse should ever be worked for at least an hour after being fed. The odd placement of a horse's stomach makes it dangerous for it to be exercised immediately after eating. When the stomach is full it places pressure on the muscles of the diaphragm, which abuts the lungs at the front and the stomach at the rear. If a horse is galloped on a full stomach, the enlarged stomach will press against the diaphragm, which will in turn exert pressure against the lungs, and can cause the lungs to bleed.

In addition, exercise will disrupt the horse's digestive processes, which are not all that efficient to begin with. A horse has a surprisingly small stomach in relation to its size. The stomach is designed to digest small quantities of food on a more or less continuous basis, which is what happens when a horse is allowed to forage for itself. A stabled horse is inevitably subject to human convenience, but it is asking for trouble to give a horse more than about four pounds of hay at a time. The horse needs time to digest each feeding before being worked. Your grandson is going to have to rework *his* schedule to keep his horse healthy.

37.
TOO MUCH FOR THE SYSTEM

Q. Our Dartmoor pony put on a lot of weight over the winter and seems quite lethargic. *Should an overweight pony be given extra exercise?*

A. No, because with all that extra poundage it will be hard on his legs. He is also likely to get winded quickly. You need to recondition your pony slowly, starting at a walk and working up to a slow trot. At the same time you will need to cut down on his grazing time. Your pony is likely to find new grass irresistible and add to his weight problem. In general, the British breeds of ponies must be prevented from eating too much grass. These breeds have spent centuries foraging in high areas where the food was fairly sparse, and their systems do not deal well with too much food.

38.

FEEDING CONFUSION

Q. I am a new horse owner who is thoroughly fed up with all the contradictions regarding what to feed a horse. Books, horse magazines, and other horse owners all have different ideas, and even when they start off sounding sensible, what follows turns into such a string of ifs, ands, and buts that it makes my head spin. *Is there any basic feeding program that is generally accepted?*

A. There are some general principles that are fairly well accepted, although everyone seems to have an individual way of stating them. Beyond that, I quite agree, you run into so many caveats that most experts end up sounding as though they are conducting elaborate exercises in covering themselves.

Let's look at why even general principles tend to fall apart:

1. Feed small amounts at a time and do it several times a day, usually five. This is the one thing just about everybody agrees on. But—and you probably don't want to hear this—this rule only applies during winter months when your horse doesn't get to graze on pasture.

2. A horse needs to be fed enough to provide the proper amount of energy for the tasks it is asked to perform. Of course, this simple sentence has one question after another built into it. What if my horse works a lot less in winter? What if I only ride on weekends? And on and on.

3. The ratio between bulk and concentrate, the former consisting of hay, the latter of concentrated grain mix, is very important. And what should that ratio be? Oh, between one-half and two-thirds bulk. Really? Try to bake a cake

according to those instructions and you'll have a disaster.
4. Water is even more important than feed. Horses' bodies
    are eighty percent water and they will run into serious
    problems quickly if they don't get enough. And then the
    list of buts starts, concerning when your horse should not
    have water.

The truth is that like human beings, every horse has a slightly,
and sometimes considerably, different metabolism from every
other. Veterinarians know this, and most vets know better than to
try to give answers that cover the vast number of situations that
may apply. Talk to your own veterinarian, who knows your particular horse or horses, and take his or her advice. When it comes
to feeding, broad generalities just don't work.

39.
MORE FOOD IN SUMMER?

Q. I have been told that horses need to consume more food
in summer than in winter. I would have thought that it was the
other way around. *What factors are involved that make it necessary to increase dietary intake in the summer?*

A. The main factor is heredity. The modern horse, even with
infusions of Arabian blood, is better adapted to cold weather than
to hot weather. In this regard, the ancestors from the high steppes
of eastern Europe and Asia hold sway. It requires a great deal of
additional energy for a horse to cool down its large body, even
with a much greater water intake. Also most horses are worked
harder in summer than in winter, whether on the farm or on the
track. If a horse's intake of food isn't sufficient for the job it is
asked to perform, the horse will draw on its own fatty tissues to
make up the difference, which will eventually be injurious.

When increasing food intake, remember that the digestive process in itself creates heat, so finding a proper balance is vital. This is a subject to discuss with your veterinarian, since dietary requirements can vary considerably from horse to horse.

40.

HUNGRY MOTHERS

Q. My mare consumed a lot more feed during her pregnancy, but I expected that. Now I am being told that after the foaling she is going to require even more food. *Why should a mare require even more feed after giving birth?*

A. Because, while nursing, she is eating for two. Additionally, she will be expending enormous amounts of energy looking

after her foal. The colt or filly is no helpless babe in arms that sleeps fifteen hours a day. It will be romping around like the dickens within hours of its birth, and the mare will be attentive to its every movement. This is a very draining time in more ways than one, and many mares will consume up to four times as much feed as they ordinarily would. The amount of feed should be gradually increased in the weeks following the foaling, and then gradually tapered off as the foal begins to wean.

41.

NATURE'S POISONS

Q. On the verge of buying my first horse, when I thought I had everything covered from stabling to pastureland, I was told that I should have a naturalist or botanist check my pasture for poisonous plants. Poison ivy I could understand, but we're talking buttercups here. Wow! *Are there really a number of plants that are poisonous to horses that I have to be on the lookout for?*

A. I had the same reaction you did when told about buttercups. But most of the buttercup family will cause horses intestinal distress, although they won't eat them unless the rest of the forage is of poor quality. For some reason, horses do seem to be attracted to the color yellow. Another gastric disaster is the yellow-flowered ragwort. Foxglove and monkshood are problems, too, and English yew is absolutely deadly.

If you have good pastureland, none of these plants should really be a problem. Cats can be poisoned by all kinds of house-plants, including those Christmas favorites, poinsettias, but the trouble with cats is that they will eat something out of mere curiosity. Horses don't do that, but trouble can arise when pastureland isn't up to standard.

42.

TETANUS TRUTHS

Q. We recently bought a small farm and are talking with a local man about purchasing one of his mare's foals for our son. One subject that came up was vaccinations, and he told us he doesn't believe in giving tetanus vaccinations to horses unless absolutely necessary. He claims that it spoils them as animals. *Aren't tetanus shots particularly important for horses because of all the manure around?*

A. There is an old superstition that still persists in some rural areas that tetanus vaccinations somehow alter the nature of the horse—a theory akin to that which some dog lovers harbor about rabies shots. Rabies shots for dogs are essential—and legally required—to protect people. There are no equivalent laws concerning tetanus shots for horses, but for the sake of horses, there really ought to be.

Tetanus is a very dangerous disease for horses, causing convulsions and death in about eighty percent of cases. The spores can be present in manure or even in soil that shows no trace of fresh manure, since the organism survives for a long time. Horses are quite prone to puncture wounds, especially of the hooves, that penetrate deeply enough to allow the spores to infect the animal. All horses need tetanus shots as foals, and periodic boosters, since the effectiveness of the vaccine gradually diminishes.

43.
TOO MANY IMMUNIZATIONS?

Q. In purchasing a horse for my son, I didn't fully realize what I was getting into. I am particularly astounded by the number of immunization shots our veterinarian says the horse must have. It seems to me that if human beings got this many shots, we'd all live forever. Although the veterinarian comes highly recommended, I can't help feeling that we're being taken advantage of. *How many diseases do horses really need to be immunized against?*

A. Just because horses look so big and strong doesn't mean that they aren't vulnerable to a long list of diseases. The big five for which most veterinarians recommend immunization are tetanus, equine encephalitis, influenza, distemper, and rhinopneumonitis (or rhino for short). Treatment requires a series of initial shots and an annual booster. In the case of tetanus, another booster will be given any time a horse is injured. Additionally, boosters to guard against influenza and rhino may be given whenever there is sufficient cause for concern, such as during an influenza epidemic.

There are three different kinds of rhino, one that causes abortion, another that causes respiratory disease, and a third that brings on an uncommon nervous disorder. Thus, an inoculation against the abortion-causing strain will be advised for pregnant mares, and horses at shows are often routinely given a booster to protect against respiratory infection.

Some horse owners balk at giving so many immunizations. But if you lose a horse because you refuse to take a veterinarian's advice, you'll find yourself in a very uncomfortable position. Just have it done.

44.

WORMS, WORMS, WORMS

Q. I have had dogs all my life and only one had a problem with worms. But now we are dealing with my teenage son's horse, and it seems to be a nonstop battle. *Why are horses so susceptible to worms?*

A. Because they eat grass on which they also defecate. The larvae are hatched in the dung and cling to grass blades. They end up back in a horse's bowel, where they mature. Of the three main types of worms that grow in the bowel the tapeworm is the least harmful. The large white round worms called *ascarids* can grow to a foot in length, but even they are not as harmful as red worms, or *strongyles,* which can be fatal in young horses. Because they actually suck blood from the horse's stomach lining, and migrate through it during their life cycle, red worms can cause very serious damage.

All of these worms are controllable with drugs, although infestation can easily recur. Regular deworming schedules should be established, but the timing should be worked out with your veterinarian, since the life cycle of worms varies according to local climate.

45.

HORSE-SICK PASTURE

Q. My two horses seem to have a continual problem with worms, despite regular dewormings. I have been told that part of the problem is that I have only one two-acre pasture, which is itself the breeding ground for the worms. *When there is only one pasture, is there anything that can be done to cut down on worm reinfestation?*

49

A. Your pasture is probably what is called *horse-sick*. The residue of droppings is causing an endless cycle of reinfection—the horses get worms, are dewormed, but then get worms all over again from the very grass they are consuming. That is why, ideally, horses should be rotated from pasture to pasture, with a given plot of land taken off-limits every couple of years.

In your situation, the only thing you can do is to make an extra effort to remove manure from the pasture. You can also harrow the manure, breaking it up so that it dries out more quickly—worms can't breed in sun-dried manure.

46.

HORSE ALLERGIES

Q. My husband complains endlessly about his sinuses, as do a number of other people I know. I try to be sympathetic but since I am unaffected by pollen, mold spores, and all the rest, I sometimes get a bit impatient with all the moaning and foaming that goes on. Now it seems the horse we recently bought has allergies, too. *Is it really common for horses to develop allergies?*

A. As a chronic sinus sufferer myself, I have some doubts about the degree of your sympathy for your husband or your horse. Yes, many horses have allergies, and they suffer every bit as much as we human wrecks do. The main problem is usually fungus in hay or other feed. It is nothing to make light of. In some horses, such molds will bring on a serious bout of colic. In others there may be a breathing problem that mimics what is called broken wind, a pulmonary disease that can put a horse out of commission for months.

Moldy hay is a major problem in the horse industry. You can't always tell what you're getting just by looking at a bale. If it's been rained on, then left out in the sun long enough, the outside will look fine—but dig down and you'll find the mold. Some funguses are virtually impossible to detect by eye. Ask other horse owners, and keep searching until you find a reputable source known for its top-quality product.

47.

TOOTH TROUBLES

Q. I am one of those people who will do almost anything to avoid going to the dentist, but as a new horse owner I have been warned to take good care of my horse's teeth. *Do horses get cavities?*

A. They can, but that's not the usual problem. Horses chew with a grinding action that causes the teeth to develop extremely sharp edges. When that happens, they cut into the inside of the mouth, which can lead to colic because the horse swallows grain nearly whole, leading to obstructions in the gut. It will also cause the horse to underfeed, causing nutritional deficiencies.

At least once a year, you should have your vet grind down the sharp edges, a process called *floating*. Since a horse's teeth grow throughout its life, floating must be a yearly procedure.

48.

COUGHING FITS

Q. My four-year-old Tennessee Walking Horse has just returned from a show where I observed several horses coughing on the last day. There are no signs that he is infected yet, but I am concerned. *Are there special precautions that should be taken with a horse that has been exposed to coughing?*

A. There's not much you can do at this point except wait and see, keeping a special eye on the horse. Coughing is fundamentally a protective mechanism designed to clear the windpipe and lungs. Horses often cough because of dust and chaff in the air, or because of an allergic reaction to mold or other allergens in hay. These conditions often exist at a show, and it could be that you have nothing to worry about. But do separate the horse from any other horses as a precaution.

Viral infections, often accompanied by secondary bacterial infection, are another matter. If your horse seems generally droopy, goes off its feed, or has nasal discharge, you should call your veterinarian. Antibiotics don't affect viruses, but they can clear up the secondary bacterial infection. The horse should be only lightly exercised, kept warm with a light blanket, and anything the horse has come into contact with, from water buckets to grooming equipment, should be carefully cleaned.

49.

THRUSH PREVENTION

Q. My horse developed a thrush infection in both front hooves. I have a new veterinarian, and he questioned me quite aggressively about horse management: did I clean the hooves daily, did I clean out the stall regularly to prevent the horse from standing in soiled straw, that sort of thing. I found it rather offensive, since I pay close attention to sanitation. We've had an extremely wet spring, and there is mud everywhere. *Can horses develop thrush as a result of standing in mud?*

A. Yes, they can, but that is really beside the point. Veterinarians tend to get quite testy about thrush because it is so often a result of poor horse management, with dirty stalls or lack of attention to hoof care being prime causes. And while standing in mud can cause thrush, there's still an element of horse management at issue here.

Granted you can't control the weather, but if it's a very muddy season, you should be paying extra attention to your horse's hooves, cleaning them after every excursion outdoors. Second, you should think about putting down a different surface in the areas around your stable where your horse spends the most time. Sand can work, although you must be sure not to feed your horse near the sand, since horses can develop sand colic.

At the very least, clean those hooves thoroughly, even if you have to do it three times a day.

50.

S P L I N T S

Q. I have a year-and-a-half-old colt that has developed splints. The horse is well fed and cared for, but I have a feeling that perhaps the colt has been trained too hard—his sire had a reputation for stamina. *Is hard training a common cause of splints in young horses?*

A. Splints can be caused by poor confirmation, and are sometimes the result of improper feeding. But otherwise the condition, which often leads to lameness and is indicated by pain and swelling on the inner side of the affected limb, is indeed the result of being trained too hard or worked too much on hard surfaces. Colts are not yet mature animals, and they must be monitored carefully for any sign of splints. The condition usually responds fully to rest and treatment. Permanent lameness is unusual, although it can be a precursor of arthritis.

51.

NAVICULAR WORRIES

Q. I recently acquired a three-year-old horse who is a delight. But at a show clinic I ran into another owner who has a horse with the same sire, and he warned me to be on the lookout for navicular disease of the hoof. *Is navicular disease really hereditary, and how concerned should I be?*

A. Navicular disease in itself is not inherited, but a predisposition to it may exist because of an inherited conformation of the hoof. In such cases, the navicular bone at the center of the hoof can receive undue pressure. To avoid pain, the horse will tend to put as much weight as possible on the toe rather than the center of the hoof or the heel. That in turn can cause other problems such as contracted heels—anyone who has ever had a leg injury knows that favoring the leg by walking in an unnatural way is likely to create pain in another area. But navicular disease can be caused by excessive work on hard surfaces, even if the horse has no inherited disposition to it. The mounted police in large cities are always on the lookout for navicular disease because their horses spend so much time on asphalt.

Although a predisposition to navicular disease can be inherited, the tendency is not necessarily passed on. And the dam as well as the sire enters into the genetic equation. Since you are aware of the possibility, keep your eye peeled for signs of a problem. If your horse appears to be placing more weight on the toe, or if he often tries to break out of a trot into a canter for no apparent reason, consult your veterinarian. Navicular disease can often be combatted with special shoeing, anti-inflammatory drugs, and in serious cases, severing particular nerves can be helpful.

52.

FOUNDER DOWNERS

Q. I had thought that I was caring for my horse very well, but she suddenly developed founder. She simply didn't want to move, and lay down in the middle of being saddled, something she had never done before. My veterinarian suspected that she had consumed too much lush pasture (it has been a very wet summer and the grass is very green). But he also said that founder can have many causes. *How susceptible are horses to founder?*

A. Founder, also caused *laminitis,* is a very common problem with horses, in part because so many things can bring it on. When a horse develops founder the *laminae* that cover the pedal bone inside the hoof become inflamed. The laminae are extremely sensitive, and, as you describe, a horse will often simply lie down to avoid the pain—thus the term founder, as in the foundering of a ship.

The causes can include eating too much rich pasture, too much grain (especially wheat and barley), and drinking too much water while still hot from exercise. Any number of disorders of the stomach can lead to founder, as can the retention of part of the placenta after foaling. At the first sign of founder, a veterinarian should be called. Until the vet arrives, you can help by cooling the horse's feet with anything from running water to ice packs to cool mud. Most horses recover completely when treated quickly enough, but it can be a frightening experience for a horse owner.

53.

FRACTURE FACTS

Q. I had thought that considerable progress had been made in saving horses that suffer a leg fracture. But it seems that every time a horse breaks down at the Breeders' Cup or in Triple Crown races, it ends up being humanely destroyed. These incidents also seem to be more frequent than they used to be in the top races. *Where do things stand in terms of saving a horse with a leg fracture?*

A. Actually, the chances of saving a horse with a leg fracture have increased a great deal. Two decades ago, all horses with serious fractures were routinely destroyed; there was nothing that could be done. The difficulty lies in the weight of the horse and the necessity of keeping the bones immobilized while they heal. New surgical techniques, new materials used both internally and in the fashioning of casts, as well as the expensive but sometimes feasible use of an immersion tank in which the horse is suspended in a saline solution, have all contributed to a greater success rate.

The severity of the fracture and its site remain all-important. Unfortunately, Thoroughbreds are particularly prone to severe fractures at especially vulnerable points. There are those who believe that Thoroughbreds are raced too often, but most in the racing community disagree. Breakdowns have always been one of the risks of Thoroughbred racing, they point out, and while the fact that so many more races are televised today may draw public attention to such incidents, fractures are no more common than before—and the chances of saving the horse have definitely improved.

54.

T O O   Y O U N G   T O   R I D E?

Q. My husband grew up on a ranch in Wyoming, and he swears he was riding by the time he was four years old. Our daughter is almost four, and although we live in a small city, he wants her to start taking riding lessons when she turns four. I think she's still too young. *What is regarded as the right age for a child to begin riding?*

A. Riding-school instructors who specialize in working with young children generally agree that most children don't have sufficient motor skills or mental concentration to begin riding until they are about five. Many refuse to take a younger child. There can be exceptions to this rule, and a child growing up on a ranch may have absorbed enough by watching to start at a younger age. But a city child will not have that experience. There are a lot of things a four-year-old can handle—you can see them whizzing around at any ice rink, for example. But riding is above all a matter of *controlling* an animal that has a mind of its own. That's asking a lot of a child less than five.

55.

A   N A R R O W - B A C K E D   P O N Y

Q. We are thinking of buying a pony for our eight-year-old daughter, who loves animals. She is, however, somewhat frail due to medical problems in early childhood, and it's important to get a pony that is gentle and easy to control. *What pony breeds are most suitable for young children?*

A. The standard answer would probably be a Shetland, which is the most popular children's pony in the world. Other

strong contenders are the American Shetland and the Pony of the Americas, a new breed developed by crossing a Shetland and an Appaloosa. The latter has been growing in popularity at a remarkable pace.

But given your daughter's situation, the best answer might be a Dartmoor, a wonderful British pony that not only has a calm and affectionate nature, but offers a special advantage—it has a narrower back than most ponies, which makes it especially suitable for younger children with short legs.

56.

IN PRAISE OF PONY CLUBS

Q. My husband and I have agreed to buy our nine-year-old son a pony. We have four acres of land and an existing barn, so stabling is no problem. My husband rode when he was young and feels he can teach our son, but I feel that he should have some professional instruction. *Are Pony Clubs a good bet for the instruction of young riders?*

A. They're terrific. Pony Clubs were first organized in Great Britain in 1928, and the American version was founded in 1954. Pony Clubs are run entirely by volunteers, so the instruction is not necessarily by professionals, but the teachers are extremely knowledgeable and likely to give more personal attention than your son might get from many professionals. What's more, Pony Clubs don't just teach riding, but all the basics of horse management, from proper feeding to veterinary information. Safety is a high priority, and all riders are required to wear helmets.

Pony Clubs also sponsor competitions and introduce members to a broad range of equestrian sports. You can be a member of a Pony Club through your twenty-first year, and a considerable number of kids stay with the organization right to the cutoff age, learning new skills all the while. With more than ten thousand members across the United States, Pony Clubs are one of the foremost means of developing responsible horse owners—people who very often become volunteer instructors themselves as adults.

57.

GETTING WHAT YOU PAY FOR?

Q. People call me a self-made man, but they're wrong. My parents were immigrants and they made me what I am. I have made a lot of money in my life, and I like to spend it wisely. My granddaughter wants a horse, and I said I'd buy one for her. But the horse she wants doesn't seem like anything special to me. She says it was love at first sight, but I could spend a lot more. *Don't you get what you pay for with a horse?*

A. Not necessarily. Many great horses have been bought cheaply and many extremely expensive ones have turned out to be duds. But that's not really the point here. The horse world is too often about pedigree and money. If your granddaughter has found "her horse" and it costs less than a lot of others, then bravo for her. It sounds to me as though she knows what's really important: the bond between rider and horse. Be proud of her good sense.

58.

WHO'S THAT ON MY BACK?

Q. My daughter has been taking riding lessons for nearly a year. She has proved a fast learner, and seems to have a natural aptitude for riding. But when I go to her riding school to pick her up, I often see novice riders who are so inept, I wonder how the horses can stand having them on their backs. *Do the horses at riding schools suffer much from having so many inexperienced riders astride them day after day?*

A. Riding-school horses certainly don't have an easy time of it. They are subjected to a great many stresses and strains, such as carrying inexperienced people of all sizes and ages. Riding-school owners do make some attempt to lessen the wear and tear by juggling the work periods of their horses, and have been known to say a given horse is lame when a particularly bad rider shows up demanding his or her usual mount. Horses also know how to protect themselves to a remarkable degree. If you watch carefully as the same horse is ridden by two different novices, you will notice that the horse changes rhythm in an effort to find the most comfortable way of bearing up under a rider. Most novice riders have neither the strength nor balance to force a horse to do what they want. In many cases, the horse is more in control of the situation than the rider. Viewed in this way, school horses are not as badly off as horses owned by experienced but nevertheless bad riders who know enough to make the horse do what they want even if it is wrong!

59.
A QUESTION OF TEMPERAMENT

Q. I am twenty-two and have been riding for seven years. I finally saved enough money to buy a horse and found a Morgan that was exactly what I wanted. I asked to have a test ride, and after it was over, the owner backed off and said that he didn't feel it was the right horse for me. He was polite about it, but I badgered him until he told me why. He said the horse had a nervous temperament and since I was a rather high-strung rider, we would be a bad match. I'm still furious. I like the challenge of controlling difficult horses. *Doesn't a nervous horse need a strong-willed rider to bring it into line?*

A. Quite the opposite, I'm afraid. It is unusual for a horse owner to blow a sale in this way, but he is to be commended for his frankness. Many high-strung (or strong-willed) riders do indeed like to deal with nervous horses. It gives them a sense of power to get their way with the horse. But what this really means is a fight between horse and rider, and that's not going to do either of them much good in the long run.

Nervous horses—and there are lots of them—respond much better to a calm, patient handler. This does *not* mean weak. Patience may be one of the greatest of all virtues, especially for a rider. A horse with a placid temperament is a much better match for a high-strung rider. The horse's calmness helps soothe the rider. We tend to think that we control the horse, but the truth is that the horse has a considerable effect on our ability to relax. Riding should be a collaboration between horse and rider, not a battle.

60.

LEASING LOGIC

Q. My son badly wants to have a horse of his own. He's sixteen, remarkably responsible, and I'd much rather buy him a horse than a car (he understands that he can't have both). Still, he will be going off to college in a couple of years. I've heard that it is possible to lease a horse instead of buying. *How easy is it to lease a horse, and does this arrangement generally work out well?*

A. Leasing has become an increasingly common way of having a horse without actually owning one. It generally works out just fine for everyone concerned if all facets of the situation are thought out beforehand and agreed to by both parties in writing.

The first thing to consider is what you want to do with the horse. Is the horse just for pleasure riding, or do you want to show him? A trained show horse is going to cost a lot more to lease—as much as $1,000 a month—than a horse that is just used for trail riding. Where will the horse be stabled? Do you have a barn on your own property, or should he remain at the lessor's stable? Full leases generally mean that you'll be stabling the horse on your property, but there are also partial leases, where the horse remains at the owner's barn. In these arrangements different parties may share in the lease and have access to the horse at designated times. When drawing up a written contract, be sure to cover the following points in separate clauses:

1. Who will pay for basic health care for the horse, including such things as deworming and vaccinations? These costs are often split, but the contract should explicitly state all veterinary contingencies.
2. Who will pay the farrier costs of reshoeing?
3. Who will provide the tack for the horse?

An experienced lessor will also want to have clauses covering the possibility of serious injury to the horse or to the lessee if a fall should occur. Don't be put off by someone who insists on discussing all possibilities—it is far better to settle such matters up front than to run into problems down the line. Be more wary of the lessor whose approach is too informal. If the lessor suggests that you deal on a handshake, look elsewhere.

It is also possible to lease a horse from a stable on a short-term basis in order to determine whether that horse is one you would like to make a longer commitment to ride.

Leasing can work, and is often the best option, but it should be taken just as seriously as leasing a car.

61.

TOO SMART A HORSE?

Q.   I'm seventeen and I've been leasing a horse for the last six months. He's a beauty, and I thought I'd really lucked out because he's been so well trained for show classes. But it turns out the judges don't like what they're seeing. My horse anticipates their commands, and starts a maneuver without my doing anything at all. *Is it possible to have a horse that is too smart for its rider?*

A.   It happens quite a lot, especially when a fairly new rider buys or leases a horse that has more showing experience than the rider. Judges do not like this because you are supposed to be controlling the horse, instead of his controlling you.

You have two options. You can try to teach the horse that it

must not move unless you tell it to. This is quite an assignment, for it essentially means retraining your horse, and he may be too set in his ways to pay much attention. The effort may be worth it, even if you don't fully succeed, for the process could teach you a lot about riding. The other option is to start working with another horse. Check your lease to see if there is a clause for terminating the contract early. Sometimes lessors are willing to let a rider make a trade, depending on what other horses are available.

When leasing or buying a horse, young riders should always keep in mind that a horse that knows the ropes extremely well can turn out to be a problem instead of an easy way to success.

62.
WEEKEND TRAINING

Q. I have been riding for ten years but have never owned my own horse until my uncle recently gave me a year-and-a-half-old colt. I spend a great deal of time with him on weekends, but I can seldom find the time to try to train him during the week, and by the next weekend it's almost like starting over again. *Why doesn't drilling a horse extensively on a weekend make up for the lack of training during the week?*

A. Because young horses get bored easily, and shouldn't be drilled for more than fifteen or twenty minutes at a time in the first place. In fact, many learn best when they are drilled every other day. But a five-day interval is far too long.

Weekend riders should really be dealing with older horses that are already fully trained. To effectively train your colt, you will have to hire somebody (or find a fairly experienced young rider who will do it for fun) to take your place for a couple of days during the week. But make sure that there is good communication between you and the substitute teacher. Nothing spoils a horse faster than getting inconsistent messages—from two different people, or the same person.

63.

A FOAL FOR A FIRST HORSE?

Q. My daughter is named for an aunt who is a very wealthy woman with a whole stableful of horses. She has told my daughter that she can have a foal when she turns sixteen next year. My daughter has taken riding lessons but really doesn't know anything about caring for horses, and neither do I. *Wouldn't we be better off with an older horse than a foal?*

A. Yes indeed. Please look this gift horse in the mouth. Training a foal is not terribly difficult, provided you know exactly what you are doing. People make mistakes with dogs, like letting them bark too much when they first find their voices, and then have a lot of trouble undoing the problem. But if you make a couple of mistakes with a foal, you can end up with a major problem. The foal is, after all, going to grow up to weigh a thousand pounds or more, and retraining a horse is a much more difficult proposition than retraining a dog.

It is difficult to say no to so generous a gift. But don't let yourself be bullied. Make sure your daughter understands what the problem is, and try to persuade your aunt to part with a mature mare or gelding.

64.

YELLING INSTRUCTORS

Q. I'm sixteen and have just begun to ride. My instructor yells at me all the time. I try very hard to do things right, but it makes me very nervous when she yells at me. It's not just me, I've heard her yelling at other riders too, boys and girls. *Do all riding instructors yell at their students?*

A. No, but it's hardly uncommon. In school you've probably found that there are teachers or gym instructors who yell and those who don't. Some instructors yell to cover up their own insecurities. With others, it's just a personality trait. Some yellers are terrific teachers, others are lousy.

You should remember that there's another side to this coin: Teachers who smile and purr at your every effort may end up teaching you very little. My own experience has been that tough teachers are better teachers. However, there's no doubt that some people get so upset at being yelled at that they tune out the instructor. Since you say that your instructor yells at practically everybody, try to remember that you aren't being singled out, that this is your instructor's style. But if you really feel you're failing to learn *because* you're being yelled at, get a different instructor.

65.

LEFT-HANDED MOUNTING

Q. I moved to Arizona from Chicago last year, and friends have urged me to learn to ride. I took one lesson and stopped because I had such trouble mounting the horse. I'm not uncoordinated and I have fairly strong legs, but I am left-handed and it is extremely awkward for me to mount a horse from the left. *Is there any good reason why a horse has to be mounted from the left?*

A.   Yes, and you're not going to like it. Horses are mounted from the left because the great majority of people are right-handed. Fine, you may say, but why can't I mount from the right? The problem is that horses are trained to be mounted from the left and if you mount one from the other side, it is likely to make the horse very nervous.

If you were to buy a horse as a yearling, and train it from scratch, it would probably accept being mounted from the right. But other riders would likely sneer in your direction including, I fear, left-handers who have managed to grit their teeth and make the extra effort involved in mounting from the left.

66.

TRAINING EXPECTATIONS

Q.   My teenage son has been riding for a year and a half, and has his own horse. So far, he has just been involved in pleasure riding, but his horse does have previous show experience, and my son wants to get a trainer and develop himself as a show rider. Unfortunately, my son is not much of an athlete; in fact getting a horse was a way of compensating for the fact that he was lousy at baseball and too small for football. *Can a good trainer really do much for someone who doesn't have much athletic ability?*

A.   First, there are plenty of people who are superb at one sport and terrible at most others. Just take a look at what happens when baseball and basketball stars play a few rounds at celebrity golf tournaments. Your son may have more ability at riding than you give him credit for. Try to get a couple of objective observers who know riding well to give you a quiet estimation of your son's potential.

If it turns out that your son really doesn't have sufficient ath-letic ability (especially in terms of coordination and timing) to be a reasonably good rider, there is not much a trainer can do to help him. There are trainers who will take on such a rider, but first-rate ones really don't want to waste their own time with such a client. What's more, if your son has unrealistic expectations about what he can achieve—and even good riders are too often prone to that kind of delusion—he's headed for a fall in his self-esteem. Praise him for what he has accomplished, but try not to let him get in over his head. It won't be easy, but it's the wiser course.

67.
GIRTH TRICKS

Q. I am thirteen and just got my first horse. I am having trouble tightening the girth when I put on her saddle. I think it's tight but then when I start to mount, it always turns out it's too loose. *What is the trick to getting the girth tight the first time around?*

A. The trick is what your horse is doing. Many horses have a mischievous habit of holding their breath when they are being saddled. That way, when they exhale, their sides return to their normal dimensions, the girth will loosen, and thus be more comfortable for the horse.

All you have to do is tighten the girth once, just as you are doing, and then walk the horse a few steps. The horse will have relaxed by then and you can tighten the girth a second time.

68.

IT'S YOUR HEAD

Q. My teenage son does a great deal of riding, but refuses to have anything to do with wearing a safety helmet. "It's not a motorcycle, Dad," he says. *How dangerous is it to ride a horse without using protective headgear?*

A. It is very dangerous, particularly for younger riders. Although reliable statistics on riding accidents have only been kept since the late 1970s, they show that forty percent of injuries sustained by younger riders are head injuries, and enough of them result in death or permanent brain damage to be taken as a major warning signal.

The use of protective headgear has always run up against vociferous protest in one field after another, from hockey to motorcycling. Too hot, too heavy, too expensive, or just plain silly say the doubters, but it all boils down to "What, me worry?" Sometimes state legislatures step in, as in the case of motorcycles. At other times, one dramatic incident changes everything, as occurred when the star Boston Red Sox outfielder Tony Conigliaro was beaned by a pitch in 1967, ending his career. The riding world is now in a period of transition, with protective helmets being required in many sporting events. The trouble is that people don't necessarily wear them the rest of the time.

Helmets come in all kinds of designs—there are even ones to be worn under a western hat. Every rider should wear protective headgear. When buying, look for the seal of the Safety Equipment Institute (SEI) to be sure you're getting one that will do the job.

69.
WHAT'S PREPOTENT?

Q. When people talk about the establishment of various breeds of horses, they sometimes describe the founding father of the line as being a prepotent stallion. *Exactly what does the term prepotent mean?*

A. It is a biological term that describes the greater capacity of one parent to pass on certain desired characteristics to its offspring. The three great stallions that are the ancestors of all Thoroughbreds, the Darley Arabian, the Godolphin Barb, and the Byerley Turk, were all prepotent horses. So was Figure, the horse that established the Morgan breed. The genetic codes of these horses were of such strength that their qualities were passed on, at least to some degree, to their offspring regardless of the mare

that carried the foal. Of course, if the mare was of exceptional quality, too, the resulting foal might turn out to be even more exceptional. The operative word here, however, is *might.* It is only in recent years that biologists have begun to understand the complexity of genetic codes, and it still is something of a mystery why a foal whose parents were both great champions may not turn out to be as great a horse as one foaled by a mare of less distinction. But that is part of the thrill of breeding Thoroughbreds—no one is ever quite sure where the next great champion is going to come from. The 1977 Triple Crown winner, Seattle Slew, for example, essentially appeared out of nowhere, and was bought very cheaply as a colt because his lineage was so undistinguished.

70.
FERTILITY RIGHTS

Q. I have a lovely filly that I use as a pleasure horse. She's now four and I am seriously considering breeding her. An acquaintance has a stallion he is willing to provide for stud service at a modest fee. *How picky should one be in choosing a stud horse for a filly that has no particular credentials of her own?*

A. Owners of purebred and show horses can get very picky indeed about pedigree or performing status, and since the stud fees are high in such cases, they have every right to be. But not all the wins or championships in the world are worth anything at stud unless the stallion is fertile. A surprising number of famous colts and fillies turn out not to be good breeding stock. If there is clear evidence that a stallion performs well at stud, as demonstrated by prior instances of producing foals, then you have something to go on.

Even though your own filly has no particular credentials, insist that a veterinarian well versed in breeding examine your neighbor's stallion. Sure it will cost some money, but far less than you stand to lose if no pregnancy results. If that were to happen, a casual arrangement with a neighbor could lead to a nasty situation marked by mutual finger pointing concerning whose horse is the infertile one. A stallion that has sired a number of foals in the past may still develop problems. For example, overfeeding can make a stallion sexually uninterested.

Also have the veterinarian take swabs from the stallion to determine whether he carries *contagious equine metritis,* a bacteria that can cause infertility in the mare he has serviced (even though he is technically fertile).

71.
ULTRASOUND TESTS

Q. From what I understand, horse breeding is a chancy business from the start, never mind the quality of foal you end up with. *How soon after mating can I find out if my mare is actually pregnant?*

A. Until the 1980s, it was a complicated business to test for pregnancy, and it could be weeks before definite results were available. Ultrasound testing has changed all that. The technique is as popular among horse breeders as it is among human beings—and with horses it is used much earlier. The first ultrasound test is often made about two and a half weeks after breeding. Such tests are not always conclusive, however, so they are repeated twice more at ten-day intervals.

On about the forty-fifth day, and then again around the sixtieth day, a veterinarian will perform a manual palpation to make certain that the pregnancy is proceeding normally. There are still nine months to go until foaling, and many more tests. Problems can arise very late in pregnancy, and your veterinarian will be keeping a careful watch until delivery.

72.

VACCINATIONS DURING PREGNANCY

Q. Our mare is pregnant with her first foal, which we're of course very excited about, but we're also quite anxious. Some people have advised us to make sure that the mare is vaccinated against tetanus and red worms in the final months, but others say that this can cause her to abort. *Is it safe to vaccinate a mare in the last months of pregnancy?*

A. The tetanus vaccination is certainly safe, and can be of great benefit if the mare should have any tearing during foaling. Vaccination for red worms (strongyles) must be done with care, since the organophosphate vaccines have been known to cause abortions. But other vaccines may be perfectly safe. Be sure to consult your veterinarian before using *any.*

In addition to protecting the mare, these vaccines offer immunity to the foal, protecting the newborn for an average of six weeks.

73.

FOALING ODDITIES

Q. I recently witnessed a mare giving birth to a foal for the first time. I didn't want to interfere, but there were some things that surprised me. For example, the mare had several strong contractions and then just lay there for several minutes. Then the contractions started and stopped again. No one seemed alarmed, but I wondered if this was normal. Also, after the foal's body was mostly on the ground, its rear feet remained in the womb for almost half an hour while the mare and foal lay quite still. *Are rest periods during labor and after most of the foal has appeared normal?*

A. Both are completely normal. The mare may also stand up after her rest period, with the next set of contractions taking place while she's standing. It is also common for the foal's rear legs to remain in the womb during the postpartum rest period. They will soon be expelled by the movement of the mare or the foal, although it usually happens when the mare first sits up to take a look at her foal.

Another aspect of foaling that often surprises first-timers is the fact that the umbilical cord is allowed to remain intact until it breaks naturally as either the foal or the mare stands up. The cord should remain attached for as long as nature allows, since the foal is receiving blood and nutrients from the mare's placenta in the half hour or so that the two rest together. Human intervention during the foaling shouldn't be necessary unless some obvious problem (such as protracted labor) occurs.

74.

VITAL EVIDENCE

Q. I have been told that after a mare gives birth, the afterbirth must be kept until it can be looked over by a veterinarian. I'm not by any means a squeamish person, but this does seem a bit much. *Why is it so important to retain the afterbirth for inspection?*

A. Because a trained eye can tell by looking whether the entire placenta has been expelled from the mare's body. An owner, trainer, or groom with ample experience can make that judgment too, but beginners need an expert opinion. If any of the afterbirth has not been expelled, the veterinarian will have to intervene to remove it, since it can cause a number of physical problems if retained.

75

75.

YEARLING MATURITY

Q. Some foals seem to mature physically at a more rapid rate than others. But, as I understand it, even a well-developed yearling may not be ready to be broken because its bone development has not necessarily kept pace with its muscle development. *What's the best way of determining whether it is safe to break a young horse?*

A. Muscle does develop more quickly than bone, a fact that causes many an inexperienced owner to break a yearling too soon. But there is a standard veterinary test for determining whether a horse is sufficiently developed. The test involves taking an X ray of a horse's knees to determine the state of the epiphyseal line, which indicates the overall skeletal maturity of the yearling. If skeletal development is slow, there will be an opening in the shaft. If this opening is large, the yearling is not yet ready to be broken. If it is partially closed, then you can proceed with breaking, but the horse should not be worked until complete fusion takes place. Some horses do mature more quickly than others, and if the shaft has completely fused, a yearling is ready to be broken and worked.

76.

BITING HORSES

Q. My horse is generally well-behaved but has a bad habit of unexpectedly biting people. *Is there anything that can be done to make a horse stop biting?*

A. It can be done, some horse owners say, but it is very difficult, and the methods vary from horse to horse. The trick is to find some small punishment that makes it clear that biting won't be tolerated. Some owners report success using everything from a short blast of mouth spray to clicking a castanet near the horse's ear. Experiment to find a method that works best for you.

Horses should really be cured of biting while they are still foals. If a foal takes a nip of the mare's teat while nursing, she gives it a bite on the rump. As the mare teaches the foal not to bite her, you can follow up by using a crop on the rear when the foal tries to bite you. Getting the same lesson from two sources simultaneously usually convinces the foal that it can't bite Mom and it can't bite humans. But if the lesson isn't taught about humans at this impressionable stage, correcting the problem later on can be a major headache.

77.

TO TREAT OR NOT TO TREAT

Q. I've been told that it's a serious mistake to bribe a horse with treats, either as a reward or to encourage them to do something. But I see people doing this, and their horses don't seem spoiled. *Is it really such a bad idea to give horses treats?*

A. There's a lot of debate on this issue. The majority of professional trainers regard the practice as anathema, but once in a while you will come across a trainer who once felt that way, but then found that giving treats worked.

Those who do give treats do it only as a reward, except possibly when trailering a horse—then a bribe can sometimes make the difference. Sugar cubes are regarded as the safest treat, because they dissolve and can't get stuck in the throat. Horses love carrots and apples, but they should always be cut up into fairly small pieces so the horse doesn't choke. If you do give treats, there will inevitably be people who look down on you, but there are also those who feel that treats really help in horse training.

78.

FIND THAT PLEASURE POINT

Q. As a lifelong dog person, I long ago discovered that every dog has a different place on its body that it particularly likes to have scratched. When my teenage daughter recently got her first horse, I suggested to her that as part of grooming her beloved Cindy Lou, she should try to find the special spot that the horse liked having scratched. *Isn't it true that horses, like all mammals, have favored scratch points that will not only give pleasure but relax the horse?*

A. There's no question about it, although horse owners who harp on tough discipline don't like to hear about it. Study after study has shown that being groomed or massaged in the right way helps mammals relax, to the point of lowering both blood pressure and heart rate. A baboon, a dog, a horse, a cat, all respond to being rubbed the right way.

The sensitive area of pleasure can differ wildly from horse to horse, and the instrument you use can make a big difference, too—for one horse, it may be a whisk broom, for another a rubber curry brush, for still another just the human hand. But once you find that spot you can use this technique for settling your horse down in tense moments—from hoof cleaning to trailer loading.

79.
UNNECESSARY ROPE BURNS

Q. I own horses and have a neighbor who does too. I often see signs of rope burn on his horses. I know better than to butt in—he is not the kind of man who listens to anybody. *But aren't rope burns avoidable if a horse is handled correctly?*

A. In the world of horses, as in life in general, genuine accidents do happen. But the fact remains that most rope burns are the result of inexperience, laziness, or outright callousness, and they are indeed largely preventable.

Rope burns usually occur on a horse's legs. To avoid this, ropes should be kept away from the bare skin on the legs. When a horse is being restrained, either leather hobbles or heavy bandages should be in place before the rope is used. All horses will try to struggle free from leg restraints, so adequate protection should be taken beforehand. While a horse may accidentally become entangled in a rope on occasion, carelessness on the part of the handler usually plays a part.

80.

A BIT THAT HURTS

Q. The horse I bought six months ago has suddenly developed an aversion to taking a bit. He tosses his head around and even tries backing away. I am an experienced rider, although this is the first horse I have owned. *When a horse suddenly gets restive about having a bit put on, does it mean there is something physically wrong with the horse or is it something that I'm doing incorrectly?*

A. It could be either. But you at least have the honesty to wonder if it could be something you are doing wrong. The horse is probably resisting the bit because of pain, and a close examination of your horse's mouth will likely reveal some kind of abrasion or dental problem. The problem could be an ill-fitting bit, or perhaps the bit is beginning to deteriorate. On the other hand, you may be handling the reins improperly. Even an experienced rider can run into problems with a new horse, such as jerking the reins more than usual to control a horse that has some bad habits or is used to being ridden differently.

Have someone you trust watch you ride. An impartial observer can often spot something that the rider is not aware of doing.

81.

COOLING DOWN

Q. Everyone talks about how important it is to cool a horse down after it has been exercised strenuously. *Can you tell the horse is cool when it stops sweating, or is there some other way to know?*

A. Sweating alone doesn't tell the whole story. When you get back from riding, put your hand between the horse's forelegs, right up against its chest. If the area feels hot, the horse needs to be cooled down, even if he isn't sweating. Put a cooler made of light wool on the horse and walk it until the chest area is at normal body temperature. A healthy horse shouldn't take more than fifteen minutes to cool down. The cooler will absorb any sweat, but the skin underneath should be dry. At that point it's safe to stable the horse.

82.
DON'T HEAT THAT STABLE

Q. We have just moved to Indiana. We're told it gets very cold in these parts in the winter, and we are concerned about our three horses, which are used to the milder weather of Maryland. *Would it be a good idea to heat the stables for the winter?*

A. No, it would not. One of the fastest ways to make a horse ill is to subject it to swings in temperature over the course of the day. With a heated stable, any time a horse goes out it must adjust to cold weather outside and then warm weather when it returns indoors, and horses are just not that adaptable. In addition, heat encourages the growth of bacteria and viruses, as well as worms.

If your horses are cold, they will shiver, in which case you can cover them with light blankets (you don't want them to sweat as that causes other problems). In general, horses like winter weather, although Thoroughbreds are not as hardy as most horses and require special attention.

FLIES UNENDING

Q. The fly population in our part of southeastern Pennsylvania seems to have exploded during the last couple of years. We have three horses and they have been suffering a lot. *Are there any special tricks to combatting flies?*

A. Your fly population problems consist of quite a number of different pests. The common housefly is prevalent everywhere. It heads straight for the mucous membranes of the horse, feasting on the secretions of eyes, nose, and mouth. Aside from causing irritation, this fly also carries *habronema,* a parasitic worm that can make its way from the eyes (where it causes conjunctivitis), to the intestines. The so-called face fly tends to dote on cattle, but it won't turn down a horse. It also often carries a worm that causes conjunctivitis.

Then there are the bloodsuckers, the stable fly, the true horse-fly, and the horn fly. Not only do they carry disease, but their bites alone can drive a horse crazy. Barely visible gnats also bite, particularly around the ears.

There are many repellents on the market for controlling pests, but overuse of these chemicals can be harmful to the horse. One trick to control gnats is to coat a horse's ears with petroleum jelly, which the gnats can't penetrate. Scrupulous sanitation, carried out on a daily basis, is the best way of controlling pests. All these flying insects (except gnats) breed in manure or soiled bedding. Sanitation is important year round, but during fly season, remove manure and soiled bedding twice as often and keep any manure piles closely covered. Without these measures, pesticide ointments aren't worth much.

84.

TRAILER TENSIONS

Q. My excitement at taking my horse to his first show sixty miles away is being overshadowed by my nervousness about getting him there—this is the first time he will have traveled by trailer. I have heard horror stories about loading horses into trailers, and I have seen people yelling hysterically at shows. *What are the most important requirements for loading a horse successfully?*

A. Patience, patience, and patience. Some horses don't seem to mind getting into trailers, others hate it. And even the ones who usually load easily can suddenly turn balky for no apparent reason.

There are those who believe that a horse should be hungry when he is loaded, and that a haynet full of hay in the trailer will then persuade the horse to step right in. Most professionals frown on this approach, largely because the horse is usually being taken someplace to perform, and a disruption of the feeding schedule is likely to put the horse off form. But even professionals are not above using a small bribe—such as a carrot—if necessary.

The main thing is to remain calm and patient. Never yell at the horse, whip him, or in any way lose your cool. He is nervous about getting in the trailer. If you get upset, he will get even more upset. If you hit him, he will come to associate the trailer with being abused, and you will have even more trouble the next time. Be prepared to try again and again to load your horse. If he won't budge, back off, lead him around in a circle and try again. Try a dozen times or more if you have to. Obviously, this means giving yourself plenty of time for the loading. The less time you have, the more likely you are to get upset.

Finally, recognize that there is a time to give up and seek help from someone more experienced.

85.

HOUDINI HORSES

Q. I have a new horse who is a regular Houdini when it comes to escaping. He seems to have an unerring instinct for locating a weak fence post, as well as a talent for lifting fence boards out of place. *What can be done to keep a horse that's an escape artist from getting loose?*

A. Many horses, and a great many ponies, seem to have some Houdini in them. Some horses actually learn to slide bolts with their teeth. One answer is an electrified fence that delivers enough current to startle the horse without really hurting him. To teach him about the fence, you must first tempt him by putting hay on the other side of the fence. After his first shock, move the hay up and down the fence so that the horse gets the idea that the whole area is booby trapped.

There are some extremely spirited horses and ponies that will say to hell with the shock and charge on through anyway. Then your only recourse is to build a wooden fence that is very strong indeed, with deep poles and immovable railings.

86.

STEEPLE TO STEEPLE

Q. I suppose that steeplechase racing is known to the average American, if at all, through the famous movie of the 1940s, *National Velvet,* which starred the young Liz Taylor. In 1990 I was lucky enough to attend the Grand National, which is still one of Great Britain's greatest sporting events. *What are the origins of steeplechasing and why has it never caught on in America?*

A. The first steeplechase occurred in 1752 as a result of a private bet between two Irish gentlemen, Mr. O'Callaghan and

Mr. Blake. The contest was staged to see which horse and rider could cover the four and a half miles between two Irish churches, the Church of St. Buttevant and St. Leger Church, in the shortest time. The spire of St. Leger was tall enough to be seen for miles, thus providing a guide to the racers, who could choose any course they liked, leaping walls, fences, and hedges in the process.

It was another fifty years before steeplechasing became an organized sport. It quickly grew in popularity, and the first Grand National was held in 1839 at Aintree, near Liverpool. There have been a number of American horses that have won the Grand National, but they have been ridden by English or Irish jockeys. As to why the sport has never really caught on in the United States, it may have something to do with how often horses fall in the course of a steeplechase, something that Americans are far more squeamish about than the English and Irish. There has been a steeplechase event included in the Breeders' Cup races since 1986, but almost all the entries are foreign.

87.
THE FIRST CLASSIC RACE

Q. Although we Americans don't like to admit it, I suppose that the English Epsom Derby is regarded as the world's premiere Thoroughbred race. *Is the Derby, first run in 1780, the oldest surviving race for Thoroughbreds?*

A. No, two other classic British races are older. The St. Leger was first run at Doncaster in 1777, and the Oaks, for three-year-old fillies, was created in 1779. All of these races were a departure from past practices. The Thoroughbred races earlier in the eighteenth century were run over much longer distances, usually four miles, and horses were not raced until they were five or six years old. Thus these three famous races set the pattern for racing as we know it today.

The first winner of the Derby was Diomed, owned by Sir Charles Bunbury. It was Sir Charles whom Oscar Wilde had in mind when he wrote his famous line for *The Importance of Being Earnest,* "I have invented an invaluable permanent invalid called Bunbury, in order that I may be able to go down into the country whenever I choose." It's not that Sir Charles himself was an invalid, but that he loathed having to spend time in London away from his beloved horses.

88.

THE AMERICAN SEAT

Q. The way jockeys ride Thoroughbreds, crouched over the withers, weight far forward, clearly has aerodynamic advantages that are beneficial to the speed of the horse. *How long has this style of riding been practiced by jockeys and who originated it?*

A. It was introduced in the United States following the Civil War, as new tracks sprang up all over the country. The so-called *American seat* was disdained by the British, whose jockeys rode sitting squarely on the horse with an erect back. The British thought this elegant style was appropriate to the sport of kings, and described the new American riding mode as resembling a monkey on a stick. When several American riders had great success with the new approach on English tracks, it was quickly taken up by British riders as well.

89.

WHEN RACING ALMOST DIED

Q. I have noticed that the number of times the Belmont Stakes has been contested does not match up with the number of years since it was first run. It's off by a couple of years. *Was the running of the Belmont Stakes suspended during World War I?*

A. No, the problem came earlier. During the early years of the twentieth century there was a huge public backlash against Thoroughbred racing, partially because of scandals involving fixed races, but largely because of a widespread moral outcry against gambling. The bookie came to be regarded as one of the foremost despoilers of the American character, and horse racing was banned in state after state. At one point it was legal only in Maryland and Kentucky, thus the Belmont Stakes was not run in 1910 or 1911, although both the Kentucky Derby and Maryland's Preakness were held.

Then, in 1908, when the moralist factions in Kentucky almost succeeded in getting the Kentucky Derby cancelled, the state took over with the introduction of parimutuel machines. Already in use in France, these machines took betting out of the hands of the bookies. With betting now overseen by state authorities and the frantic efforts of the racing community to clean up other abuses, Thoroughbred racing quickly regained its good name. Though problems crop up occasionally, racing is now so heavily monitored that it is widely regarded as one of the cleanest of all sports.

90.
WHAT'S IN A NAME?

Q. I am the kind of Thoroughbred racing fan who watches the Triple Crown on television and goes to a track once or twice a year more as an outing than to bet or to study the sport. To me, one of the most colorful aspects of the sport is the fanciful names owners come up with for their horses. *Are the sometimes very odd names of Thoroughbred race horses just a tradition or is there some specific reason for them?*

A. There is a specific reason. Every Thoroughbred you see race, whether in England, France, the United States, or anywhere else is descended from one of three stallions taken to the British Isles at the end of the sixteenth century. They were called the Byerley Turk, the Darley Arabian, and the Godolphin Barb. Since bloodlines are absolutely essential to both breeding and handicapping racehorses, the overseers of the sport long ago decreed that no name could ever be used twice, ruling out any possibility of confusion. This means the owners must use their imaginations and ingenuity to come up with names that are new and still attractive to racing fans (a lot of fans put great weight on names when placing a bet).

There's another rule involving names that also limits choice: No horse may have a name that is longer than eighteen letters, including the spaces between words. That's why you see names like Itsallgreektome, winner of the 1990 Hollywood Turf Cup. If the words were separated by spaces, the total spaces would number 19—justnotpermissible!

91.

JOHN HENRY IS HIS NAME

Q. I'm not a rabid animal rights person, but it always disturbs me when I watch one of the major televised races, like the Kentucky Derby, and hear that one of the horses is a gelding. I don't really understand why anyone would castrate a racehorse. *Isn't it true that even great horses make more in stud fees than they ever made racing?*

A. To begin with, you probably would not be seeing that gelding running in the Kentucky Derby at all if he had not been castrated. You are correct that stud fees can bring in a great deal of money, and no racehorse is gelded without good reason. In the majority of cases, the colt is simply too aggressive or wayward to succeed as a racehorse. Castration settles the horse down sufficiently so that it can be trained and raced. Additionally, there are colts that are so sexually over-active that they can't be entered in the same race as a filly—they try to mount her long before they get to the starting gate. Finally, there are a number of physical problems involving genital function that can indicate castration for the good of the colt's health.

Gelding a horse can certainly have its financial rewards on the track. The great John Henry won a total of $6,597,947, second only (by a mere $82,000) to Alysheba. He raced for years longer than any modern stallion because there was no temptation to retire him to stud.

92.

HANDICAP HORSE SENSE

Q. Maybe it's just my luck—or maybe I don't go to the track often enough to know what I'm doing—but I always seem to do worse betting on handicap races. Handicapping seems to me more of an art than a science, anyway. *How long has handicapping been used in Thoroughbred racing?*

A. The first significant handicap race was the running of the Outlands Stakes at Ascot in 1791. But the modern system for handicapping, as well as the weight-for-age scale, were not devised until nearly seventy years later. They were the work of Admiral Rouse, who was the handicapper for Britain's Jockey Club beginning in 1855.

Handicap races generally involve older horses. There is no handicap in any of the Triple Crown races, for example. Some horses may have to carry a little weight because of the lightness of the jockey so that all the horses go off at the same weight. For a handicap race involving four- and five-year-old horses, horses are rated by ability (according to their previous records) and age, with the assumption that an older horse is a stronger horse. The object of handicapping is to ensure that all the entries begin the race with an equal chance of winning. It is certainly as much an art as a science, but it does encourage bettors to spread their money across the field of entries.

93.

A HORSE BY ANY OTHER COLOR

Q. I have a friend who always bets on gray horses at Thoroughbred races, everything else being equal and even sometimes when it's not. Another friend refuses to bet on a black horse under any circumstances. *Is there any rational basis whatsoever for betting according to a horse's color?*

A. Nope. Such behavior is sheer superstition—which can be a far more powerful force than reason. Horses come in four basic colors: black, brown, bay, and chestnut. Any other color, including gray, roan, white, and mixtures like the pied or the Appaloosa must be patiently bred into horses. An unwillingness to bet on a black horse may grow out of the same fears that make many Americans nervous about black cats. The gray is a more interesting case. Unlike a roan, for example, which is born that color and retains it, grays are one of the four basic colors when they are foaled. Their color changes as they mature. To some, this process carries with it an element of the mysterious that is associated with good luck.

Very few people are totally objective when it comes to color, shutting it out of the betting equation altogether. Back in the 1970s, a horse came onto the track that I hadn't considered betting on. It was a striking animal, a dark red roan with an almost purple undertone, and it had a beautiful mane and tail. Its name was Peony, and the name was so wondrously appropriate that I made a breakneck run to put down a two-dollar bet before the windows closed. Peony won the race, at odds of 17–1. I was saved from fixation by the simple fact that I have never again laid eyes on a horse that color.

94.

LASIX ARGUMENTS

Q. My father was recently prescribed Lasix for his mild congestive heart condition. I told him he would no longer be allowed to race on New York State tracks. He was amused, but then we got into a discussion of why this drug can be used for racehorses in some states and not others. *Is there any real proof that Lasix improves the performance of horses enough to warrant a ban?*

A. The guardians of racing in various states regularly get into serious snits over this issue. It gets a fresh and noisy hearing every spring during the Triple Crown races, since the use of the drug is allowed in Kentucky and Maryland but not in New York. If a horse wins the Kentucky Derby or the Preakness, or even places well while running on Lasix, the trainer is subjected to endless questions from the press about whether the horse will be entered in the Belmont Stakes where it will have to run without it. Some trainers go ahead, others keep the horse out of the Belmont. Lasix is used to control bleeding of the throat that affects some Thoroughbreds during or after a race. A trainer's decision about running a horse without Lasix usually depends on how serious a problem the horse has. Some trainers use the drug largely as a precaution; others feel it is essential to protect the health of their horse.

As to whether there is any proof that Lasix really improves performance, the short answer is no. But the long answer is that the racing stewards of New York and some other states point out that there's no proof that it doesn't. On top of that, there is a certain amount of circumstantial evidence that it can give a horse greater speed, stamina, or just that something extra.

95.
A QUARTER MILE TOO FAR?

Q. I love to watch the Triple Crown races in the spring. Because of the different lengths of the three races, it is very difficult for a single horse to win them all. That's fine by me, because it makes those horses that do take the Triple Crown all the more special. *Was there a decision to run the Kentucky Derby, the Preakness Stakes, and the Belmont Stakes at different lengths, or did it just turn out that way?*

A. The lengths of these races has been the same since their inception. Many people are unaware, however, that the calendar order in which they are run is exactly the reverse of the order of their founding. The Belmont Stakes was first run in 1867, at one and a half miles (Belmont Park, where it takes place, did not open until 1905, though). The Preakness was first run in 1873, then as now at Pimlico, and the Kentucky Derby was inaugurated at Churchill Downs in Louisville two years later. The Kentucky Derby has become the most legendary of the three races, perhaps because the winners of the other two are so often surprises. Many people believe the one-and-a-quarter-mile Kentucky Derby is the truest test. The slightly shorter Preakness, at one mile, one and a half furlongs, favors early speed, while the length of the Belmont demands additional stamina.

There are many racing experts who feel that the three races are too closely bunched together, taking place in a mere five weeks, and that for the good of the horses they should be more widely spaced, perhaps over a period of two months. Traditionalists balk at any change, however, feeling that it would compromise the integrity of the historical record. It's the same sort of problem that developed when Roger Maris surpassed Babe Ruth's single-year home run record—since the number of games played had been increased, could he really be said to have topped the Babe? The baseball powers eventually came to the conclusion that the longer season, one involving extended jet travel, was in fact tougher than what Babe Ruth had to contend with. But if the Triple Crown calendar is changed, you can be sure that any future Triple Crown winner will be stigmatized as "no Secretariat."

96.

LIGHT ON THE ECLIPSE AWARDS

Q. At the end of every racing season, I read in the newspaper about the Eclipse Awards for the top Thoroughbreds in various categories, including Horse of the Year. *Why are they called the Eclipse Awards?*

A. They are named for one of the most famous horses in the history of racing. Eclipse, a British stallion, was a great-great-grandson of two out of the three horses all Thoroughbreds are descended from, the Byerley Turk and the Darley Arabian. Eclipse was foaled on April Fool's Day in 1764, during a complete eclipse of the sun in northern Europe. He didn't begin racing until he was five years old, in May of 1769. Over the course of the next two years, he ran twenty-six times and was never defeated. The great English animal painter, George Stubbs, did a famous portrait of Eclipse in 1786.

97.

LATE BLOOMERS?

Q. Every year it seems that at least two or three horses that weren't even entered in the Triple Crown races show up late in the season and suddenly start beating Kentucky Derby or Preakness stars. Sometimes there's even a horse that doesn't make that much of a showing until it is four, and then starts winning race after race for older horses. *Are these horses that win big when they're older just late bloomers, or is there something else involved?*

A. There are other things involved. For starters, in Thoroughbred racing, all horses are considered to have been born January first. In order to point toward the Triple Crown races, horses usually need to start racing in the fall of their second year. Some colts and fillies may be several months younger than other horses that are technically the same age. They are simply not mature enough to race as yet, and are held back. Thus they will miss out on the Triple Crown races, but when they do begin racing, fully mature and much fresher than their older competitors, they can absolutely dazzle, and leave a public favorite that began racing earlier in the dust.

There is a small but vocal minority in American Thoroughbred racing who feel that no horse should be raced until it is three years old, as is the case in Great Britain and Europe. They don't think there should be any such thing as Breeders' Cup races for Juveniles and Juvenile Fillies. Such trainers and owners, though few in number, do get to grin a little wider when the horse they held back charges past a Kentucky Derby winner in the final stretch.

98.

HOW MANY THOROUGHBREDS?

Q. I go to races at Aqueduct or Belmont Park in New York a couple of times a year. When I do I buy a copy of the *Daily Racing Form* just for the fun of it. The listing of the entries at various tracks always seems kind of stunning—keeping track of the pedigrees of so many horses must be an enormous task. *How many Thoroughbreds does such information exist for?*

A. All those that ever raced. The first stud book was published in England in 1791, and an American listing was begun in 1873. By 1896 the American version of Britain's Jockey Club, located in Lexington, Kentucky, took over the task for American Thoroughbreds. The number of horses for which the Jockey Club has pedigree histories is now edging toward two million.

It's usually a good deal easier to trace a Thoroughbred family tree back to the eighteenth century than it is a human one.

99.

SARATOGA SPECIAL

Q. The Triple Crown races seem to get the most media attention, but the Travers Stakes at Saratoga Springs, New York, every summer seems to me to be just as exciting, and often has more to do with the naming of the Horse of the Year. *When was the first Travers Stakes run?*

A. It was first run in 1864, three years before the first Belmont Stakes. The Saratoga season has always held a very important place in American racing, not least because it has always drawn members of society. You are correct that the Travers has in the past had great influence on the choice of the Horse of the

Year, because it is open to both the three-year-olds that compete for the Triple Crown and to older horses, often including one or more of the previous year's Triple Crown winners. In recent years, however, the establishment of the Breeders' Cup in the late fall has diminished the importance of the Travers as a benchmark for Horse of the Year.

100.

BATTLES OF THE SEXES

Q. Racing fans get all excited when a filly is entered in the Kentucky Derby, but it seems to me that a filly would have a better chance in the shorter Preakness. *Haven't more fillies won the Preakness than the Kentucky Derby?*

A. Yes, four fillies have won the Preakness and only three the Kentucky Derby. However, the last filly to win the Preakness was Nellie Morse in 1924. The Kentucky Derby has had more recent distaff winners with Genuine Risk and Winning Colors in 1980 and 1988. The mile-and-a-half Belmont Stakes has been won by only two fillies, the last being Tanya back in 1905.

Quite a few trainers are against the idea of entering a filly in the Triple Crown races no matter how good she appears to be. This is because there is a Triple Crown for fillies, consisting of the Champagne, Acorn, and Mother Goose Stakes, all run at Belmont Park.

IOI.

TRUE SHOWMANSHIP

Q. I have friends who rush off to New York every time the famous Lippizaners from Vienna come to the city to perform. The Lippizaners are wonderful, but I keep telling these people that there's an even showier horse right in their own back yard. All they have to do is go to the country horse show to watch American Saddlebreds strut their spectacular stuff. *Am I being chauvinistic in thinking the American Saddlebred is the most spectacular show horse in the world?*

A. Not at all—I agree with you. Both breeds have their devotees. The Lippizaners have a lot of romantic appeal because the breed goes back for centuries and has so much history connected with it, including the effort to save them from the Nazis.

Lippizaners have enormous stately grace, but many horse lovers do prefer the liveliness of the American Saddlehorse and its almost balletic quickness.

American Saddlebreds (also called Kentucky Saddlers) were bred by Southern plantation owners from a mixture of Thoroughbred, Morgan, and Narragansett Pacer. They are a superb riding horse, but the majority are now pointed toward the show ring. The breed has three natural gaits, a walk, a trot, and a canter, and two gaits they are trained to, the slow gait and the rack. The rack is a four-beat gait elevated into another realm by the fact that each foot pauses briefly in mid-air before being set down. It could stand as the definition of the word ''prance,'' and is thrilling to watch.

102.
RACING IN HARNESS

Q. Thanks to a new boyfriend I have just discovered harness racing. There's only one problem. He likes the trotters best and I prefer the pacers. *Are trotters and pacers different breeds of horse or are they trained differently?*

A. Both are American Standardbreds that are trained differently. However, certain lineages tend to produce horses that are better suited to one or the other of these forms of harness racing. The American Standardbred has a remarkably mixed heritage that includes Thoroughbred, English trotting horses, the famous Hackney of Great Britain, as well as some Arabian and Morgan blood. The most important progenitor was Hambletonian 10, one of the most prolific sires of the mid-nineteenth century in Great Britain. His ancestor, the Thoroughbred Messenger, brought to the United States in 1788, also played a major role in the development of the breed.

Pacers and trotters each have their own Triple Crown series.

The pacer races consist of the Cane Pace, the Little Brown Jug, and the Messenger Stakes. For the trotters it is the Yonkers Trot, the Kentucky Futurity, and the most famous of all harness races, the Hambletonian, in which each horse must run in two separate heats. The trotting Triple Crown began in 1955, the pacing version a year later; there have been six trotting Triple Crown winners, none since 1972. The pacers can boast seven winners, the latest in 1983.

In order to be allowed to race, trotters must demonstrate that they can cover a mile in two minutes and thirty seconds, and pacers must do the same in two minutes and twenty-five seconds. As to the question of preferring trotters to pacers, it is largely a matter of aesthetics. The trotters go a little faster, which some people find more exciting, but the pacers have a more elegant action, which provides a different kind of thrill.

THAT LADY IS A JOCKEY

Q. Men and women have been competing directly with one another in equestrian events nationally, internationally, and in the Olympics since the end of World War I. A lot of women have won against men, too. *Why has it taken so long for women to gain a foothold as jockeys in Thoroughbred racing?*

A. The same prejudices, old-boy networks, and closed-shop attitudes have been prevalent in Thoroughbred racing that have held women back in so many other professions. The first woman jockey to come to real national attention in America was Robyn Smith in the 1970s, but she quit the sport to marry Fred Astaire. Since then, there has been a gradual increase in the number of women jockeys and as of 1993, one has finally gotten to the very top of the profession. Julie Krone had quite a year in 1993, as she became the first woman jockey to win a Triple Crown event, taking the Belmont Stakes aboard Colonial, and then went on to become only the third jockey ever to ride five winners in one afternoon in the 126 prestigious years of the Saratoga Springs Summer Meet in upstate New York. The previous jockeys to accomplish the feat were racing immortals Angel Cordero, Jr., and Ron Turcotte, and no one had done it in twenty years.

But even as she was achieving these successes, there were articles pointing out that there are large numbers of women working in Thoroughbred racing who are still stuck at the lower positions of groom and exercise boy. Julie Krone's ascendance is bound to help.

104.

BLACK JOCKEYS

Q. Although some of the greatest jockeys come from a Hispanic background, including Eddie Belmonte, Braulio Baeza, and Angel Cordero, you almost never see a black jockey. *Have there ever been prominent black jockeys in Thoroughbred racing?*

A. There were quite a few well-known black jockeys in the years between the end of the Civil War and the turn of the century. One of the greatest riders of the time was Isaac "Ike" Murphy, who had a total of 1,400 mounts during his career, and won an astounding forty-four percent of the time. No modern jockey has ever achieved so high a winning percentage.

There have been some complaints about the paucity of black jockeys, but the low numbers of black managers in baseball and black head coaches in football tend to get the publicity. There are a considerable number of African-Americans involved in Thoroughbred racing, and as the number of black owners of race horses increases, it is likely there will be more African-American jockeys and trainers who make a national impact.

105.

OLYMPIC RIDING

Q. Although they seldom get much television coverage, the equestrian events are among my favorites in the Summer Olympics. *How far back in Olympic history do equestrian events go?*

A. In terms of the modern Olympics, equestrian events were first included at the second Games, held in Paris in 1900, but they were certainly a part of the ancient Olympics, beginning at the 23rd Olympiad in 688 B.C., when four-horse chariot racing was introduced. Mounted riders competed for the first time at the 33rd Olympiad in 648 B.C. Despite the collapse of the Greek Golden Age, the Games continued throughout the course of the Roman Empire. They were finally banned in A.D. 393, by the last emperor of the united empire, Theodosius I, a Christian, who was attempting to stamp out the last vestiges of paganism. The Olympics, even at that late date, were dedicated to the Greek god Zeus.

The chariot races of the ancient Games must have been as spectacular as those depicted by Hollywood in *Ben Hur*. The Greek poet Pindar noted that at the start of the fourth century B.C., a single race was contested by forty charioteers.

106.
CROSSBRED JUMPERS

Q. Show jumping is a sport that I find particularly appealing, not just because of the heart-in-the-mouth tensions involved, but also because so many of the horses are absolutely beautiful. *Are most show jumpers Thoroughbreds, or are they a cross with some other breed?*

A. Some are Thoroughbreds, but the majority are horses that have been crossbred. This has little to do with their appearance, however. Most show-jumping horses are just getting going in competition at an age when the majority of Thoroughbred race horses have already been retired to stud. As more mature animals, show jumpers have filled out in ways that many horse lovers find especially appealing.

The reason why crossbred horses are preferred for show jumping is that they are less skittish than many Thoroughbreds, whose high-strung temperament makes them ill-suited for the psychological rigors of jumping. These days several breeds of German horses predominate in the show-jumping world, in part because of the great success of German riders in international competition.

Hanoverians and Holsteins are particularly popular with American riders.

107.

JUMPING BLIND

Q. Whether being ridden while hunting, or competing in the three-day event, horses seem to have a natural aptitude for jumping. But I have heard people say that jumping is in fact an unnatural thing for a horse to do. *Why would jumping pose any particular difficulty for a horse?*

A. Because of the way a horse's eyes are positioned in its head. Horses have splendid lateral vision, and even, when the head is sufficiently lifted, a degree of rear-view vision. Focusing on what is directly in front of them is more difficult, and generally accomplished by turning the head slightly so that one eye is focused ahead.

If you watch a jumping competition closely, concentrating on what each horse's head is doing, you will notice that good riders allow the horse considerable freedom of head movement. Otherwise the horse would be jumping almost blind. Riders also approach jumps so that a horse can get a good lateral look at the obstacle before the turn is completed into a straight-on approach. Given the problems of vision involved, together with the complex and subtle communications necessary between rider and horse, it is remarkable that there are as few spills as there are.

108.

JUMPING TOWARD HOME

Q. I have noticed that in jumping and cross-country equestrian events, many of the most difficult obstacles come toward the end of the course. This seems odd to me—surely horses would do better if the most difficult jumps were taken at the beginning, when the horse is freshest. *Is there a good reason why the highest or broadest obstacles are often placed toward the end of the course?*

A. Yes, and it has to do with one of the deepest of equine instincts—to herd together. Horses feel most secure in the company of other horses, and they have a strong basic urge to return to whatever place horses are gathered together, whether in an enclosure or a particular field. Thus many course designers take advantage of this instinct by placing the most difficult jumps at a point where the horse has the sense that it is returning to the paddock or collecting ring where other horses are gathered. The urge to return to the group is so strong that a horse will draw upon all its resources to surmount the obstacles that stand between it and a reunion with others of its kind.

109.

DRESSAGE ORIGINS

Q. There seem to me few more elegant competitions than those devoted to the art of dressage. The precision with which the horses perform their complex maneuvers, and the poise of the riders is wonderful to watch. *Is it true that dressage was originally developed for largely practical reasons by European armies?*

A. The practice of dressage can be traced back much farther than that, as we know from surviving Greek texts written in the fifth century A.D. The word dressage, originally French, doesn't make its appearance until the eighteenth century. It means, to quote the *Dictionary of Borrowed Words,* "the training of horses to obey commands and perform precise maneuvers." In the eighteenth century those particularly interested in training horses to obey were indeed military men, for this was an age in which the cavalry was of paramount importance.

The fundamentals of dressage were codified in the early eighteenth century by François de la Guerinière. Throughout the previous few centuries, the training of horses had been debased and brutalized, but Guerinière restored the value of patience and aesthetics that had been originated by the Greeks. His concepts were adopted by Vienna's Spanish Riding School and remain basic to contemporary dressage competition.

110.

THE THREE-DAY EVENT

Q. Having moved from Chicago to Virginia, I have been introduced to the pleasure of attending three-day events as a spectator. *What are the origins of this demanding sport?*

A. The three-day event, consisting of dressage, cross-country, and jumping, has ancient roots. In 300 B.C., the Greek military commander Xenophon first described the qualities of training and horsemanship essential to the three-day event. But the first modern competition was held by the French cavalry in 1902. Military units in other countries took up this test of complete horsemanship, and it was first included in the Olympics in 1912. But it was not until after the Second World War that competition was opened to civilians.

The three-day event always begins with the dressage competition, followed by the cross-country course; the horses return to the arena for the jumping test. The reason for this order has nothing to do with horsemanship itself, but is intended to keep the public interested. Since spectators cannot be easily accommodated on the cross country course, the first and last events are held in an arena.

111.

AN ANCIENT GAME

Q. I keep running into people who insist that polo was invented by the British. I think they've just seen too many pictures of Prince Charles falling off his horse. *Isn't polo one of the world's most ancient sports?*

A. Yes, it is. Its exact origins are unknown, but it existed in Mongolia, China, and other parts of Asia more than two thousand years ago in one form or another. Specific mention of it dates back to the time of Alexander the Great (356–323 B.C.), when the sport was played by the Persians. It was not played in England until 1869, when it was brought back by English officers who had seen it in India. Despite the costs involved in maintaining polo ponies, the sport became popular not only in England but also in the United States and Argentina, where the breeding of polo ponies became an important equestrian pursuit. The first international competition was held in 1886.

Given the great speed of the game, its quick stops, and the need for precise turns, polo ponies must be able to perform more maneuvers well and under greater stress than almost any other kind of horse. A top polo pony needs as much as two years of rigorous training.

112.
RODEO ROOTS

Q. When my son was eight years old he decided that he wanted to go to the rodeo at Madison Square Garden. Rodeo is great entertainment, and we're about to make our fourth outing. One of the things I like about it is that it seems to reflect the challenges faced by actual working cowboys despite all the pageantry. *How much of what goes on at a rodeo really harks back to the actual work done by cowboys a century ago?*

A. The only two events that are truly rooted in the working cowboy's daily routine are the calf roping and tying, and bronco riding. But even the bull riding and steer wrestling grow out of contests that cowboys staged at the end of a trail drive, when they had some money to bet and some bragging to do. Informal riding and roping events sprang up after the Civil War, and a few formal contests were held in the late 1870s. The spread of the railroads and the stringing of barbed wire across endless stretches of the western landscape brought the trail driving days to an end in the 1880s, but by then the western legends were already very much a part of the American consciousness. Beginning in 1883, Buffalo Bill had a great success with his touring Wild West show, which featured the sharpshooter Annie Oakley and for the 1885 tour, the chief who defeated Custer, Sitting Bull.

As the years went on, the modern rodeo developed. The cowboys who compete for prize money pay their own way and ride their own horses, and their recurrent injuries are very real indeed. Even the clowns serve a purpose by distracting the bulls from fallen riders. Perhaps it is the sense that rodeos are in fact connected to a real past that makes them so popular, not only in the United States, but on tours to the far corners of the world.

113.
REINING TRAINING

Q. I have been riding for two years, and am thinking about buying a horse. A man I know slightly is pressing me to buy a reining horse he owns. The horse is twelve years old. *What special qualities about a reining horse might make it a good buy for a fairly new rider?*

A. What your acquaintance is trying to sell you is a highly trained, competitive horse. Reining contests have their roots in the jobs performed since the post–Civil War cattle drives, and grew in popularity and over the years, with organized competitions becoming more prevalent. The National Reining Horse Association took such competitions to another level when it was formed in 1966. The contests involve a combination of athleticism and control that is remarkable, and requires both strength and precision on the part of the horse. The majority of competing riders have their horses trained by professionals. No matter how good

the training, the horse will only perform up to the ability of the rider to communicate what is wanted.

Although reining horses (most of which are American Quarter Horses) are remarkably controllable, a plus for a fairly new rider, they also require a very knowledgeable rider to get the most out of them. I would strongly suggest attending a reining contest before you make any decision. In order to be happy with such a horse, you will need some special training yourself. Even kids are getting involved in reining contests these days, and there is no reason why you can't handle it. But you should be prepared to meet some new riding challenges. A twelve-year-old horse should be well settled down, but you should still try to acquire skills to match *his* abilities.

114.

THE PLEASURE CLASS

Q. I have acquired a horse that I am told has considerable show potential. Since I am a novice when it comes to showing, I am uncertain what discipline to concentrate on. *What is the usual route for a beginner to take when entering shows?*

A. It usually makes most sense to begin by showing in the pleasure-horse class. For one thing, every breed association sponsors a pleasure class, and because the discipline is not as specialized, a less experienced horse and rider can still do quite well. Judging is based on performance, manners, suitability to the rider, and conformation of the horse, in that order of performance. In many cases, even horses that are being pointed toward a more specific discipline are first introduced to the show ring in pleasure classes. A pleasure class can give both you and your horse experience and additional clues as to what more rigorous discipline might be suitable down the line.

115.

CIRCUS HORSES

Q. My favorite acts in circuses are always those involving horses. The animals are so beautiful and the stunts their acrobatic riders perform are thrilling. But one does wonder how well these horses are treated. *Are circus horses trained humanely and properly cared for?*

A. There are few horses in the world that are so lovingly cared for as circus horses. It takes years to train a star horse, and such training requires immense patience and an almost telepathic understanding of the mind of the horse. I assure you that circus horses lead extremely privileged lives and, unlike Thoroughbred racehorses, are never asked to exceed their physical limits.

116.

OVERCONDITIONING

Q. I have a friend who has show horses, and my own mostly Morgan pleasure horse is stabled at the same barn. My friend got me caught up in conditioning programs that she puts her show horses through, but it is my feeling that my horse is more difficult to ride now that he is in peak condition. *Is it possible to over-condition a horse?*

A. It most certainly is! Horses should be conditioned to the point at which they perform the tasks expected of them with ease, and they should be cooled down fairly quickly afterward. If a horse is conditioned beyond that point—which varies a lot from discipline to discipline—the horse is going to be keyed up to a degree that will make it jumpy, even fractious, if it isn't allowed to make full use of the energy it has stored up.

A pleasure horse should never be conditioned to the same degree as a Thoroughbred or a show horse. You can even go too far with hunting horses and with special kinds of show animals like reining horses, which have to be able to stop and stand very still and appear relaxed. Not only is an overconditioned horse not going to be as happy performing the more modest or more specialized tasks expected of it, but, like retired professional athletes, can actually lose tone because of insufficient activity. The extent of a conditioning program should always be in proportion to performance goals.

117.

A BREEDING INVESTMENT?

Q. I have a chance to join a group of friends in buying a filly that did quite well racing as a two-year-old, winning a couple of allowance races and coming in third or fourth in secondary stakes races. The idea is to race her for one more year and then to breed her. *Is a middling filly a good investment in terms of future breeding fees?*

A. The same statement once made about backing Broadway musicals is equally applicable here: "It's a lot more fun than most ways of losing money, and once in a while it actually works out in your favor."

Horses, like Broadway shows, are way up at the top of the "big risk" category. A new show can have hot stars, writers with great track records, and the genius director of the moment, and still close before it officially opens, or mere days after the opening. Horses, even those that seem poised for greatness after their first racing season, can fade to the status of also-rans or, worse, break down while running, succumb to disease, and leave one saddened and out a lot of money.

Nor do great horses necessarily become great sires or dams. The beloved Genuine Risk, the 1980 Kentucky Derby and Eclipse Award winner, either miscarried or had stillborn deliveries for a decade, until she finally produced a healthy foal in 1993. For all mares, the infertility rate for any given year is around 25 percent. On a more optimistic note, middling fillies, like the one you are considering investing in, do occasionally prove to be exceptional mares. In the end, putting your money into the ownership of horses is in itself a genuine risk. It can be very rewarding, financially or otherwise, but never invest more than you can afford to lose.

113

118.

UNWANTED HORSES

Q. My thirty-five-year-old daughter and I are having a fairly friendly debate, although I'm not certain it's going to stay that way. She has a six-year-old mare she has owned for two years. It's a very nice riding horse, but nothing special. Nevertheless she wants to breed the mare, so that her children can have the experience of watching a foal grow up. She says she will then sell the colt or filly. *Isn't it true that there are more horses available than can easily be sold?*

A. Yes, there are. It's not the staggering problem that exists with cats and dogs, but there are quite a lot of unwanted horses around, and too many of them end up getting sold to a slaughterhouse.

There are always a few breeds that are in vogue at any given time where the demand outstrips the supply. But breeding an ordinary pleasure horse without being prepared to have the offspring around for another quarter-century verges on irresponsible. Professionals with exceptional horses in their barns know when to cut back on breeding Thoroughbreds, as has happened in the past few years when the recession cut into both the prices and the number of horses sold at Kentucky's famous Keeneland Sales. When the professionals are concerned enough to cut back, the amateur certainly ought to pay attention.

119.

HORSE ABUSE

Q. The small farm next to mine was bought by a city slicker who then bought a horse that he is clearly abusing. The poor horse is terrified of him and is of course becoming less and less manageable, and thus gets whipped even more. I know I should report what's going on to the authorities, but my neighbor frightens me. *Is there anything one can do to stop animal abuse without getting personally involved?*

A. You are in a difficult situation. Even if you send an anonymous letter to the ASPCA or the police, your neighbor is going to suspect you because you live next to him. Fortunately—or from another point of view unfortunately—the police tend to deal better with animal abuse cases than they do with reports of child abuse. The abuser is seen as an owner rather than a parent, and there is less reluctance to step in.

A lot depends on what your local situation is. You should probably start by contacting the offices of the nearest horse association, regardless of the breed of your neighbor's horse. Go in personally and explain the situation and your fears. If you are lucky, the association may take on the problem.

120.

SUED BY TRESPASSERS

Q. I own a farm that is surrounded by other farms. But the largest of them all, just a mile and a half down the road, has recently been sold for a housing development. Of course I don't like seeing the countryside spoiled, but that is not my main concern. I have four horses on eleven acres of land, which should be far more than enough. *But how can I protect myself from people, particularly children, getting onto my property and then having the parents sue me because the child is in some way injured?*

A. The problem you are facing is on the increase all over the country. Many horse owners have been sued by people who think that the best way to get rich in America is to go to court. In one case a five-year-old girl climbed through a barbed wire fence that was posted with many no-trespassing signs, and she was kicked in the head by a horse she approached from the rear. The case took three years to reach a resolution, with the Kentucky Supreme Court finally throwing it out.

Where were the child's parents? you may ask. Liability laws vary from state to state, and they are often vague or contradictory. I would strongly suggest seeking advice from an attorney who specializes in equine law. You may have to upgrade fences, post more signs, or take other protective steps, but this can save you money in the long run. And the fact that you did make a real effort to prevent a problem would stand you in good stead should you ever be sued.

121.

AN EQUESTRIAN COLLEGE

Q. My sixteen-year-old daughter is mad about horses and has decided that she wants to be either a veterinarian or a trainer. She has seen ads in horse magazines for colleges that offer degrees in equestrian science and preveterinary courses. *Are colleges that offer degrees in equestrian science to be taken seriously or are they just glorified summer camps?*

A. There are a number of smaller colleges offering equestrian science degrees that are very serious places. Some also offer

Bachelor of Arts degrees that can be combined with a minor in equestrian science. Preveterinary courses are very difficult and demand academic excellence. For the young person who wants a career in the equestrian world, such colleges can be a very good bet. Write to the admissions office at a number of them and compare their curricula. At the same time it might be advisable to request information from some colleges that do not offer equestrian courses in order to get a broader picture. Your daughter is presumably in her third year of high school. It's not too soon to start investigating the possibilities.

122.
COMPANIONSHIP WANTED

Q. At a family gathering over the Christmas holidays, we announced that we were planning to buy a horse for our daughter. A curmudgeonly uncle immediately started grilling us on where we were going to keep it, how often it would be exercised, etc. We told him that we were going to fix up the small barn on our property and that the horse would be exercised every day. The uncle asked, "Just the one horse?" We said yes, and he said that was plain cruelty. *Is it true that horses really require the companionship of other horses?*

A. It has become quite a common practice for people to keep a single horse on their property, and they don't like to hear what your uncle is saying, but he's right. Dogs attach themselves completely to their owners, and cats would just as soon have any territory to themselves. However, horses need other horses. Even with all the inbreeding that has gone on over the past couple of centuries, the herd instinct remains very strong. A horse that lives by itself is not going to pine away, but it is likely to become neurotic in one way or another.

When told this, people often ask if the family dog or cat won't help keep the horse company. Depending on the particular dog or cat—and the horse—this can help; there are many nice stories about such friendships. But this is only a partial solution. People often get a lot of satisfaction out of saying, ''I have my own horse, right in the backyard,'' but frankly they are being selfish. The horse will be happier and thus a better mount if some kind of group stabling can be arranged. At the very least, the single-horse owner should try to provide a goat, easily cared for and an excellent companion for horses, to alleviate loneliness.

123.

THERAPEUTIC RIDING

Q. My daughter was paralyzed from the waist down in an automobile accident. A friend has suggested that she would benefit from horseback riding and says there are organizations that specialize in therapeutic riding. The whole idea frankly scares me. *Can a paraplegic really ride a horse safely?*

A. Absolutely. Even quadriplegics are enrolled in some of these programs. Therapeutic horseback riding is far more common than most people realize—there are nearly five hundred therapeutic riding centers in the United States. They are found in all fifty states and most states have several. The great majority are nonprofit, funded by donations and grants, and staffed by a small army of volunteers as well as certified instructors.

The last thing you need to worry about is the safety of your daughter. Volunteers are at hand every moment to make sure that no one falls off. Therapeutic horseback riding does wonders for the psychological wellbeing of disabled or handicapped people. In addition, rehabilitation experts regard horseback riding as one of the very best forms of physical therapy. I assure you that you will be thrilled at your daughter's pleasure in riding.

124.

NEW HOMES FOR OLD HORSES

Q. My mother, a widow in her early sixties, has terminal cancer. She has always been a courageous woman, and is much more concerned about what will happen to her two older show horses on her Vermont farm than she is about herself. I live in New York City and my brother lives in Brussels, so we must find alternatives. *What options are there for finding a new home for horses more than fifteen years old?*

A. While it's unusual for a horse to remain healthy beyond the age of twenty-five, that still gives your mother's horses ten years of life and perhaps more. Older horses, especially ones with special training in an equestrian sporting field, can be just what a teenager or even an older novice needs. Try to sell the horses—or even give them away—to someone in the market for a first horse. But please do this through personal contact with veterinarians, trainers, or other horse owners. Do not put an ad in a newspaper unless you are planning on asking at least $1,500 for each horse. There are a lot of unscrupulous people around who say they will take good care of a horse they can get cheaply, then sell it to a slaughterhouse that will pay them something in the neighborhood of $700. Horse meat is much in demand as a gourmet delicacy in both Europe and Japan.

Another possibility is to donate the horses to nonprofit programs for the disabled or disturbed young people. Many of these programs do yeoman service, and are always in need of horses. If your mother's horses were even older, a retirement farm would be an option, although the majority of these require a monthly fee, and they should be thoroughly explored to determine how well they really look after their animals. From what you say, your mother might be particularly amenable to the idea of her horses' being employed in a therapeutic program.

125.

THE GREATEST OF THEM ALL?

Q. My grandfather and I have a disagreement. I believe that Secretariat is the greatest of all American racehorses, but he insists that it's Citation who also won the Triple Crown back in 1948. *Is there any general agreement about the stature of the most famous American racehorses?*

A. None whatsoever. Both Secretariat and Citation have their adherents, but Man o' War, winner of the 1920 Preakness and Belmont Stakes (he didn't race in the Kentucky Derby) will also get a lot of votes. Then there are the advocates of Native Dancer and Nashua, both of whom came in second in the Kentucky Derby, in 1953 and 1955, but went on to win the other two races and become great sires of countless champions. Some will even insist upon Alydar, second to Affirmed in all three races in 1978; they hold that those three seconds, never achieved by any other horse, betoken a gallantry of spirit unequaled in the history of American racing.

Personally, I would vote for Secretariat, for the simple reason that I was there when he won the Belmont Stakes. His track record still stands, and he became the first Triple Crown winner in a quarter century. I had made my way down to the edge of the track two races earlier on that June day in 1973, and was standing by the rail about a hundred yards beyond the finish line when Secretariat came pounding down the track, his nearest competitor so far back as to be no more than a distant blur. I will never forget the enormous roar of the crowds behind me in the stands, nor the sight of that magnificent creature charging past as though he could have run the race all over again right then and there. It was the most thrilling sports experience of my life.

BIBLIOGRAPHY

Brown, Dee. *Bury My Heart at Wounded Knee.* New York: Henry Holt, 1970.

Dobie, J. Frank. *The Mustangs.* Boston: Little, Brown, 1952.

Edwards, Elwyn Hartley, Ed. *Encyclopedia of the Horse.* New York: Crescent, 1990.

Edwards, Elwyn Hartley. *The Ultimate Horse Book.* New York: Dorling, Kindersley, 1991.

Edwards, Elwyn Hartley, and Candid Geddes, Eds. *The Complete Horse Book.* North Pomfret, Vt.: Trafalgar Square, 1988.

Ensmiger, M. E., Ed. *Breeding and Raising Horses.* Washington, D.C.: United States Department of Agriculture, 1982.

Hapgood, Ruth. *First Horse.* San Francisco: Chronicle, 1972.

Harris, Catherine. *Practical Pony Keeping.* New York: Arco, 1978.

Hawcroft, Tim. *The Complete Book of Horse Care.* New York: Howell Book House, 1989.

Horses, Horses, Horses. London: Hamlyn, 1962.

Malone, John Williams. *An Album of the American Cowboy.* New York: Franklin Watts, 1971.

Osborne, Walter D. *The Quarter Horse.* New York: Grosset and Dunlap, 1977.

Phillips, Lance. *The Saddle Horse.* New York: A. S. Barnes, 1964.

Pittinger, Peggy Jett. *The Back-Yard Foal.* Cranbury, N.J.: A. S. Barnes, 1965.

Price, Eleanor F., and Gadwell M. Collins. *Basic Horse Care.* New York: Doubleday, 1986.

Ritvo, Harriet. *The Animal Estate.* Cambridge, Mass.: Harvard University Press, 1987.

Seth-Smith, Michael, Ed. *The Horse.* London: Octopus Books, 1979.

Silver, Caroline. *The Illustrated Guide to Horses of the World.* Stamford, Conn.: Longmeadow Press, 1993.

Smith, Donald J. *Horses at Work.* Wellingborough, England: Patrick Stephens, 1985.

Treasury of Horses, London: Octopus Books, 1975.

Watts, Peter A. *A Dictionary of the Old West.* New York: Promontory Press, 1982.

Welsh, Peter C. *Track and Road: The American Trotting Horse.* Washington, D.C.: Smithsonian Institution Press, 1967.

INDEX

contracted heels, 54
cooling down, 44, 55, 80–81, 112
Cordero, Angel, Jr., 101, 102
coughing, 51–52
cowboys, 16, 28, 108–109
cross-country events, 105, 107

Daily Racing Form, 96
Dances with Wolves, 15
Darley Arabian, 71, 88, 94
Dartmoor pony, 42–43, 58
Diomed, 86
disorders, 46–56
    allergies, 50–51, 52
    arthritis, 53
    bleeding of the throat, 92
    broken wind, 50
    colic, 16, 37, 50, 51, 53
    conjunctivitis, 82
    contagious equine metritis, 73
    contracted heels, 54
    coughing, 51–52
    distemper, 48
    equine encephalitis, 48
    founder (laminitis), 55
    influenza, 48
    leg fractures, 56
    navicular disease, 54
    poisonous plants and, 46
    puncture wounds, 47
    rhinopneumonitis, 48
    splints, 53
    tetanus, 47, 48, 74
    thrush infections, 52–53
    tooth problems, 51, 80
    vaccinations for, 47–48, 74
    viral infections, 52, 81
    worms, 49–50, 81, 82
distemper, 48
donkeys, 26–27
draft horses, 21–22, 23
    pulling power of, 13
    war horses as, 22
dressage, 98–99, 106, 107
    saddle for, 34

ears, laid-back, 26–27
Eclipse, 94
Eclipse Awards, 94, 113
electrified fences, 84
English yew, 46
Eohippus, 9

Epsom Derby, 85–86
equestrian science, 116–117
equine encephalitis, 48
Equus caballus, 9
escape artists, 84
Europe, 9, 11, 23, 95, 106, 120
    cold-blooded horses of, 10, 41, 44
    Great Horses of, 21–22
evolution, horse, 9, 10–11, 28, 29, 44
exercise, 41–43, 55
    conditioning, 112
    cooling down after, 44, 55, 80–81,
        112
    after feeding, 41–42
    of overweight ponies, 42–43
Exmoor pony, 41
extinction, 11–12, 24

face fly, 82
farriers, 31–32
feed bin, 38
feeding, 41–46, 50–51, 53, 73, 83
    of Arabians by Bedouins, 16
    basic programs for, 43–44
    exercising after, 41–42
    of nursing mares, 45–46
    of overweight ponies, 42–43
    stomach and, 42, 55
    in summer, 44–45
    see also grazing; hay
fences, 116
    barbed-wire vs. wooden, 39–40
    electrified, 84
fertility, 72–73, 113
Figure, 18, 71
fire branding, 33
flies, 82
floating, of teeth, 51
foaling, 46, 74–75
    afterbirth in, 55, 75
foals, 20, 45–46, 47, 72, 74, 91, 113,
    114
    biting by, 77
    as first horse, 66
    founder (laminitis), 55
    foxglove, 46
    fractures, leg, 56
    France, 87, 106, 107
    freeze branding, 33

gaits:
    of American Saddlebred, 99

Lasix, 92
lawsuits, 115–116
leasing, 62–63, 64–65
leg fractures, 56
leg restraints, 79
lip branding, 33
Lippizaners, 98–99
Little Brown Jug, 100
loneliness, 41, 117–118

Man o' War, 121
mares, 19, 54, 71–75, 114
   fertility of, 73, 113
   foaling by, 46, 55, 74–75
   nursing, 45–46, 77
   see also pregnancy
Maris, Roger, 93–94
memory, 12
Messenger, 99
Messenger Stakes, 100
Middle East:
   breeding of Arabian in, 15–16
   development of riding in, 9
   hot-blooded horses of, 10
Misty of Chincoteague, 29
moldy hay, 50–51, 52
Mongolian Wild Horse (Przewalskii),
   10–11
monkshood, 46
Morgan, Justin, 18
Morgan, 18, 71, 99
Mother Goose Stakes, 97
mounting, 67–68
mules, 27
Murphy, Isaac "Ike," 102
Mustangs, 27–28, 29, 31

names, Thoroughbred, 88, 91
Narragansett Pacer, 99
Nashua, 121
National Reining Horse Association,
   109
National Show Horse, 25
National Show Horse Registry, 25
National Velvet, 84
Native Americans, 11–12, 15, 27
   Appaloosas bred by, 16–17
   Mustangs of, 27, 28
   Pintos of, 21
   rawhide boots employed by, 31
Native Dancer, 121
navicular disease, 54

Nellie Morse, 97
nervous horses, 61–62
New Forest pony, 41
Nez Percé Indians, 16–17
North America:
   extinction in, 11–12
   Spanish horses introduced in, 11,
      16–17, 19, 24, 27
nursing mares, 45–46, 77

Oaks race, 85
older horse, new homes for, 119–120
Olympic riding, 102–103
Omar Pasha, 16
Outland Stakes, 90
overconditioning, 112
overweight ponies, 42–43

pacers, 99–100
Palominos, 25–26
paper, as bedding material, 37
Paso Fino, 23–24
pastures, pasturing:
   horse-sick, 49–50
   poisonous plants in, 46
   year-round, of Shetland ponies,
      40–41
   see also grazing
Patton, George, 27
peanut shells, as bedding material, 37
pedigrees, 96
Percheron, 23
Persia (Iran), 9
Peruvian Paso Fino, 24
piebalds, 21, 91
pied, 91
pigs, intelligence of, 12
Pindar, 103
Pintos, 21
pleasure class, 111
pleasure points, 78–79
poisonous plants, 46
Poland, 11
polo, 107–108
ponies, 10, 57–59
   British, 41, 42–43, 58
   height of, 30
   overweight, 42–43
   Palomino, 26
   Shetland, *see* Shetland pony
   suitable for young children, 57–58
   wild, on Assateague, 29

Pony Clubs, 59
Pony of the Americas, 58
Preakness Stakes, 92, 93–94, 95, 97,
    121
pregnancy, 45, 73–75, 113
    abortion of, 48, 74
    ultrasound tests for, 73
    vaccinations during, 74
    prepotent stallions, 71–72
Przewalski, Colonel N. M., 10–11
Przewalskii (Mongolian Wild Horse),
    10–11
Puerto Rico, 23
puncture wounds, 47

Quarter Horse, American, 18–19, 26,
    110

racing, 84–97
    American Quarter Horse, 19
    branding and, 34
    chariot, 102–103
    harness, 99–100
    steeplechase, 84–85
    Thoroughbred, see Thoroughbred
        racing
rack, 99
ragwort, yellow-flowered, 46
rearing bit, 35
red worms (strongyles), 49, 74
reining horses, 109–110, 112
reins, 80
retirement farms, 120
retraining, 65, 66, 79
rhinopneumonitis, 48
riding, 80
    appropriate age to begin, 57
    athletic ability in, 68–69
    bareback, 13
    jockey style of, 86
    Olympic, 102–103
    origination of, 9
    on Paso Finos, 23–24
    protective helmets for, 70
    show, 68–69
    temperament in, 61–62
    therapeutic, 119, 120
    unnaturalness of, 13
    weight distribution in, 13, 34
riding instructors, 57, 59
    yelling by, 67
riding-school horses, 60–61

roans, 91
rodeos, 108–109
Rogers, Roy, 25
Romans, 30, 103
rope burns, 79
Rouse, Admiral, 90
rubber horseshoes, 31
Russia, 11, 16
Ruth, Babe, 93–94

saddle blankets, 34
saddles:
    girths of, 69
    shapes of, 34
    "tree" of, 15
St. Leger race, 85
sand colic, 53
sanitation, 37, 50, 52–53, 82
Saratoga Springs, N.Y., 96–97, 101
Seattle Slew, 72
Secretariat, 94, 120–121
selling, 114, 120
    of Assateague ponies, 29
Shetland pony, 10, 57, 58
    year-round pasturing of, 40–41
Shire, 21
show horses, 33, 35, 48, 51–52, 83,
    98–99, 119–120
    conditioning of, 112
    leasing of, 62, 64–65
    in pleasure class, 111
show jumping, 35, 103–104
show riding, 68–69
skewbalds, 21
slaughterhouses, 120
Smith, Robyn, 101
snaffle bits, 35
Spain, 11, 16–17, 19, 24, 27
Spanish Riding School, 106
splints, 53
"spooking," 39
stable flies, 82
stabling, 36–38, 63
    heated, 81
    requirements for, 36, 37
    sanitation of, 37, 52–53, 82
    year-round pasturing vs., 40–41
stallions, 19, 54, 71–73, 88, 94, 99
    fertility of, 72–73
    gelding of, 89
    prepotent, 71–72
steeplechase racing, 84–85

127